STAYING ALIVE!

Cookbook for
Cancer Free Living

Real Survivors...Real Recipes...Real Results

STAYING ALIVE!

Cookbook for
Cancer Free Living

Real Survivors...Real Recipes...Real Results

Sally Errey

stories by **Trevor Simpson**

First Edition

Belissimo Books
Vancouver, Canada

Staying Alive! Cookbook for Cancer Free Living
Real Survivors...Real Recipes...Real Results

Sally Errey, with stories by Trevor Simpson

First Published in 2004 by:
Belissimo Books
Box 46838
Vancouver, British Columbia
V6J 5M4, Canada

National Library of Canada Cataloguing in Publication Data

Errey, Sally
Staying alive! : cookbook for cancer free living : real survivors—
real recipes— real results / Sally Errey ; stories by Trevor Simpson.

Includes index.
ISBN 0-9732987-0-7

1. Cancer—Diet therapy. 2. Cancer—Diet therapy—Recipes. I.
Simpson, Trevor. II. Title.
RC271.D52E77 2003   616.99'40654   C2003-910896-1

Edited by: Sandra Tonn
Art Director: Terence Yeung
Photography: Edmond Fong, John Blackie reprinted with permission, alive Publishing Group.
          and Rod Luey Photography (c) 2003
Food Stylist: Sally Errey

Printed in Canada

Dedicated to:

my mother, Angela, for sharing her original, whole foods wisdom and

my father, John, who taught me the values of service and integrity and,

my husband, Adrian, for his strong shoulders to lean on.

Acknowledgements

A wise proverb says "It takes a whole village to raise a child", and I certainly feel that as I reflect on those who have contributed to the success of this book and supported me in so many ways.

Firstly, deep gratitude goes to every single person at the Centre for Integrated Healing who collectively provided such fertile soil for me to experience love, grow and flourish. For those very special people, Brad, Signy, Pat, Mel, Jack, Dennis, Marie and Robert who allowed your stories to be shared - your ongoing inspiration to others is beyond measure.

Many people helped create this book. Trevor Simpson not only provided the survivors stories, but gave gentle guidance and kept my spirit buoyant when it became dim. Sandra Tonn also did more than edit the book. She transformed it into something tangible, both in my mind and my reality. I am grateful for her generosity, friendship and professionalism. Warm gratitude is extended to Terence Yeung for his patient assistance in designing the book and Raymond Chung for his vibrant illustrations. Edmond Fong's gentle humour always makes a photo shoot fun and I would like to thank him for providing such professional finishing touches to each photograph. His work appears courtesy of alive Publishing Group. For all those who said "You can do this!" - my friends Adrian, Dennis, the CPI Club members, Jen Deane, Rod Luey, Harm Dhillon and all those supportive people, too numerous to mention. Thanks to the recipe testers and proof-readers for helping to polish the final product. And always, influencing me behind the scenes, more than they'll ever know, my mentors, Robert Allen, Mark Victor Hansen, Dan Poynter and Denise Michaels.

I am also aware that I am simply standing on the shoulders of those who have led the way in empowering people to heal. Pioneers like, Dr Andrew Weil, Dr Neal Barnard, Dr Roger Rogers, Dr Michael Murray and Dr Hal Gunn. The humblest of thanks go to my personal heroes, Howard Lyman and Ramtha, for teaching me to believe in me.

In closing, I would like to acknowledge all the courageous people living with cancer, and those who have passed on. Thank you for shining your light. This book is for you.

Sally Errey

Table Of Contents

Foreword

Nourishing ourselves and our loved ones involves a major expenditure of time, energy and inspiration. We spend many hours collecting or growing our food, preparing it to be eaten, eating it and then cleaning up afterwards. Add to this the substantial cost of food during a lifetime and we begin to realize the great importance of food in our lives.

Twenty years ago, the "experts" told us that there was no relationship between nutrition and cancer. Nutritionists have since dispelled the fallacy of this notion. Sally Errey focuses on the very important role of healthful nutrition in patients with cancer. Trevor Simpson has done a beautiful job preparing eight compelling case histories showing how each person overcame his or her problem with cancer through good management and sound nutrition.

A very important contribution of "Staying Alive! Cookbook for Cancer Free Living" is the emphasis on "wholism" in our daily lives-looking at all the things that support our health and healing – quality nutrition, regular exercise, quality sleep, healthy lifestyle and a positive attitude. Although the book is dedicated to the subject of cancer, its emphasis is just as important for anyone who has a desire to be well and to stay well.

Sally has succeeded in making the sometimes complicated subject of nutrition easier for all of us to understand. She has provided more than 100 recipes to ease the transition from less wholesome foods to a complete, nourishing diet. Also invaluable is the list of 20 "cancer-conquering foods" and a "Nutritional Top 40". Sally not only shows us how a nutritious diet can help to restore our health, she takes the extra step to show that sound nutrition can be a means of preventing disease, by "optimizing our immune system."

The contents of this book make us fully aware of powerful marketing systems that encourage the public to make unhealthy choices in the marketplace. The information motivates us to take a common-sense approach to food and helps us to avoid the pitfalls when exploring new foods and recipes. Tips and details about kitchen equipment help make food preparation more efficient and enjoyable. The importance of organic foods, the risks of processed foods, how to cook food and how to plan menus are all included.

This book is far more than a cookbook. In short, Sally has created a very important blueprint for upgrading nutrition and healthy living. Her lively approach and sense of humour make for easy-to-understand and enjoyable reading and referencing. "Staying Alive!" is a "must read" for not only the lay person or those with cancer, but also for physicians and nutritionists who work with people with cancer.

Thank you, Sally, for your contribution to the community's well-being.

R H.Rogers M.D.
Co-Founder, Centre for Integrated Healing

Chapter One:

Real Survivors...
Real Recipes...
Real Results

Wholism for cancer management and prevention

Everyone wants health. Most people have the desire and ability to achieve it, but few of us have the knowledge and resources for successfully implementing healthful change.

There is increasing confusion with regard to diet and food choices. Fad diets have focused on complex numbers and percentages, and it seems no one can agree on the correct figures for optimum health. Our nutrition education is limited to sensationalist exposure in the news media or from corporations with vested interests and advertising dollars that influence our daily food choices both directly and subconsciously.

The greatest need at this time is a return to a common sense approach to food. A style of eating where a fork, not a calculator, is required. Where portions can be generous and there's no need to master percentages or nutrition labels. A return to natural sources for nutrition helps us focus on foods as nature provides. Oranges come with their own wrapping and have no nutrition labels!
The structure and content of this book provides inspirational stories from those people who have "survived" their cancer, either by going into remission, achieving "spontaneous healing" or who are simply living a full, vital and active life with their cancer.

Based on my experience, helping thousands of people understand how their food choices affect their health, I have included step by step instructions for implementing healthy food choices and building immunity on a daily basis. Instant dramatic dietary change is attainable for some people, but for most it is a process of transition. Rather than focusing on eliminating "bad" foods, this book reveals the magnitude of adding powerful healing and cancer fighting foods first, and reducing potentially damaging foods second.

In order to make healthful choices we need comprehensive education on the latest cancer-fighting foods. The Top 40 cancer fighting foods are listed and clearly explained so they can be purchased and incorporated into delicious, satisfying meals.

Adopting a healthy diet is easy! If you already buy food each week and eat every day, you're 80 percent there! This book features new shopping lists and a Balanced Meal Wheel, which assists you in making meals and snacks that are optimally nourishing and disease fighting, in just three easy steps.

Changing foods and lifestyles can be overwhelming, fortunately in this book, you'll find more than 100 recipes. Each of them tried and tested with proven results. Imagine being let into the kitchen of someone who has survived their cancer, listening to their story, receiving their words of wisdom and in addition to that, receiving their precious cancer-fighting recipes! Each of our survivors has contributed their favourites, whether they have been perfect for family potlucks, decreased nausea after chemo or boosted energy.

Maybe you've tried new foods and recipes before on your own, and I have to admit, there can be plenty of opportunity for disaster. Not understanding weird ingredients and trying to cook new foods from scratch without recipes or hints from the chef can lead to bland, boring and sometimes inedible results. This book will help you avoid these pitfalls. Everything you need is now collected in one place and ready for you to start straight away.

What is cancer-free living?

Imagine your body being strong and in a stable condition for upcoming treatments or surgery. Foods nourish us at a cellular level, with fats, proteins vitamins, minerals, phytochemicals and nutrients we don't even know about yet. With the information in this book you can take charge of how your body feels and potentially influence the outcome of your treatment, maybe even shorten a hospital stay through improved healing capacity.

Cancer-free living is focusing on the whole person. Whether a tumour exists or not, there are many parts to the whole and it is the experience and quality of life of that person that counts. This differs dramatically from the traditional medicinal tumour-centred approach of eradicating the tumour. All too often, at the cost of the body's own defense system. Alternatively, in a whole-person approach to healing, the person, or "self", plays a fundamental role in healing and recovery. Although surgery, radiation and chemotherapy can play a role in cancer treatment from this perspective, it is the person, or "self", that is the focus of care, and every effort is made to enhance the patient's well-being and immune system, and support their mind, body and spirit in the healing process. Personal empowerment and self-care is honoured and supported, and participants are encouraged to explore various options and make choices that are right for them. This is the model of cancer care at the Centre for Integrated Healing, and we believe it is the model of the future of cancer care.

For more information on this approach visit the Centre's website via www.stayingalivecookbook.com/links.

Imagine supporting your immune system on a daily basis and feeling your body's innate ability to heal kicking in. People following the recommendations revealed in this book have reported more energy, better sleep, easy weight management, reduction in headaches and body pains, less sugar cravings and regular bowel movements – whether they have cancer or not.

In addition, you can fully enjoy your food, knowing that it is in-line with healing and nourishing your body. Better yet, you can go back for seconds without even a pang of guilt! In fact, the more healing foods you eat, the better you'll feel and the stronger you'll be. What a pleasant change!

Live your potential

Of course, no one can guarantee the outcome, but through our daily food and lifestyle choices we can aim to enhance the quality of life and boost our potential for health.

The secret is, I believe the body can heal itself. If you break your arm, it starts to heal immediately, not once it's in a cast or when we take some vitamins. Ultimately, it is our responsibility to provide that healing environment on a daily basis. No one can do that for us. As we will see in each survivor's story, a healing environment isn't just about food. A healing environment might also contain healthy relationships, visualizations, a positive attitude, body and energy work and exercise.

The biggest challenge you might face is managing the energy and enthusiasm that comes from re-experiencing health and vitality, let alone observing the role of your mind and having a deeper spiritual connection.
The chapters that follow describe in detail, your roadmap to regaining health: what to buy, why to buy it, how to use it, sample daily menus and tasty recipes. Remember, some of these recipes aren't just my philosophy but real recipes from real survivors. Dietary and lifestyle change worked for them and it can work for you too.

It's time for you to invest in yourself. Don't throw your health away. Make cancer-free living your number one priority and experience the results, one bite at a time.

Sally Errey, R.N.C.P.
Registered Nutritional Consultant, Practitioner
Vancouver, Canada

Chapter Two:
Pat Gordon's Story

Pat Gordon's Story

Pat was not unfamiliar with fear. In fact, she has faced so much of it in her life that her experience and techniques to deal with it head on led her to a successful career as a speaker on the subject. She inspired hundreds of groups in the '90s with her respected teachings about "Facing Your Fears" and "How To Make Your Own Luck." Pat believes passionately that, for better or worse, we create our own lives. Yet none of her personal experiences, her time dealing with five frisky grandchildren, travelling the world for decades or her unwavering positive thinking had prepared her for the shock of a diagnosis of cancer.

In October of 1998 she discovered a lump in her breast. Her general practitioner was very encouraging and expressed confidence that there was no major problem. She had an ultra sound together with a preliminary biopsy, and while the results indicated that the lump was benign, there was some uncertainty about the findings. Further needle biopsies and ultra sounds were carried out. It was only after a procedure to remove the tumour that the diagnosis changed.

On February 2nd 1999, GroundHog day, Pat was diagnosed with cancer. The sky crashed down and she wondered if the sun would ever shine again. She found it difficult to eat, impossible to concentrate and very hard to sleep. She had a tremendous urge to climb into bed and pull the covers over her head. This journey was to be the greatest test of her personal beliefs in her life so far.

Ironically, the very next evening she was booked to give a "Facing your Fears" talk to the Newcomers Club in North Delta. Her initial reaction was to cancel the engagement, but how could she betray everything she believed in and let these people down? She pulled herself together and prepared for the experience. Imagine the drama of that presentation as she told her hushed audience that she was facing the greatest personal battle of her own life. "It was one thing to tell them that I was going to use my 'mind games' to treat my cancer. It was quite another to face up to some of the pressure I felt to take conventional treatment."

The next two days were a blur of overwhelming fears. The surgeon wanted to set a date to remove more tissue from her breast. Her family, friends and doctor were all pushing her to move ahead and there was both chemotherapy and radiation to consider. During this time, her sleep was fitful and interrupted by dreams of ghost-like figures who charged her face until she awoke in a terrified sweat with her heart racing. It was time to use some of the tools that she had used so effectively in the past.

Pat turns to the power of her inner guidance when there is an intense battle waging between thoughts and feelings. One of the techniques that works for her is to write a dialogue asking questions with her right hand and allowing her inner guide to answer them with her left hand. It was during this process that she discovered what was causing her confusion. She had a deep aversion to both chemotherapy and radiation and realized that if she did not believe in her treatment it would not heal her. It was time to seek some alternative healing options.

While visiting her local health store to enhance her regular program of vitamins and supplements she learned from the store owners about Dr. Roger Rogers who specialized in the complementary healing of cancer. This word of advice brought her to the Centre for Integrated Healing where she found that the Centre's philosophy towards healing cancer was in alignment with her own healing journey. "I felt empowered to make decisions about my own healing," she remembers, and resolved to refuse any treatment that would diminish her immune system. She had absolute faith that she could help her body heal itself.

With a goal of good health, Pat was committed to using all the tools she had been teaching others to create positive lives. She re-read a book called "The Magic of Believing," by Claude Bristol. She also re-read Dr. Andrew Weil's "Spontaneous Healing" and "Eight Weeks to Optimum Health," both of which she found inspiring and helpful. These books, as well as the information provided by the Centre in their "blue book," became sources for her to heal by-both mentally and physically. Additional tools for healing included visualization, journal writing, post-it notes and positive affirmations.

Each day Pat would fill a foolscap piece of paper with two affirmations: "I am a very healthy person," and "My immune system works very well." Her desire was to imprint these messages into the very tissues of her body. Daily walks were another opportunity to recite these affirmations in her head-over and over again, in time to her footsteps. She avoided negative thoughts by playing a cassette tape of positive affirmations and made a conscious effort to eliminate negative people and influences from her life. She read positive biographies about inspiring people and watched the renowned A&E series of the same name. She sought out stories of fellow cancer sufferers who had experienced spontaneous healing and was surprised and encouraged. Pat's conviction and experience that the power of the mind can affect the body served her well. She never thought of herself as sick, but as healthy. Her journey brought her back in touch with her spiritual side and she gave thanks every day to God for healing her.

In addition to successfully testing her often taught tools and beliefs, Pat learned some new and less obvious elements about healing. For example, she found that by forgiving all who had hurt her in the past, she was better able to heal. "It was hard to shed my wounded ego," she said, "But working on my healing without this added load was very satisfying." She is also dedicated to a new bedtime healing routine. This valuable hour involves immune system-enhancing exercises, isometrics, breathing exercises, visualization and stretching. Something else she added to her healing journey was the benefit of sharing.

"I had heard that belonging to a support group lengthens the life of cancer patients significantly."

She joined five other cancer survivors at the Centre, some of whom have become life long friends. "No façade, no frills, just themselves," she says of the group, "All chasing down a pathway to life."

July 12th 2000 became a memorable day on Pat's healing journey when her radiologist declared her free of cancer. She was not surprised. She had been convinced that she was healed for several months. It had taken her 18 months to achieve her goal of health. Convinced that her body and her immune system like it, she has not changed her new lifestyle one bit. "I feel as healthy and frisky as a flea. It is easy to remember that I can be anything that I want to be. Healthy or sick. Sad or happy. It's all up to me," she says.

Today, Pat's presentation on facing your own fears is more powerful than ever. Like many others who experience cancer, she sees the gift in her cancer and her opportunity to share her story with others.

MORE DIETARY DETAIL...

Old Favourites: Pat has understood the relationship between food and health for more than 30 years and previously ate very healthfully. She links her cancer cause mainly to stress.

Top Five Diet (and Lifestyle) Changes:

- Cut out butter

- Cut out cheese

- Added more organic foods

- No coffee

- Breathing exercises, daily walk and affirmations

No. 1 Recommendation: Read Dr Andrew Weil's books, *Spontaneous Healing* and *Eight Weeks to Optimum Health.* Visit **www.stayingalivecookbook.com/books**

Chapter Three:

Dennis Thulin's Story

Dennis Thulin's Story

Despite looking healthy at the age of 70, Dennis was not overly surprised that he had been diagnosed with cancer. "I really shouldn't be here at all," he says "I was constantly exposed to many carcinogenic materials before anyone realized just how dangerous they were."

Dennis spent most of his working life exposing his body to a variety of toxic substances, first as a heavy duty diesel mechanic and then for 30 years as the supervisor of repairs and maintenance for a couple of tow boat companies. At times he was literally swimming in PCBs while doing boat repairs, breathing in exhaust fumes in enclosed spaces or dousing his hands in dangerous cleaning chemicals. However, for most of his life, Dennis was a living example of what a remarkable healing machine the body can be.

The elements of work and life did add up, however. He had been retired for four years when in November of 1999 a biopsy indicated that he had prostate cancer with a PSA level of 1.5. At first he was depressed and felt like a victim. But, within a couple of weeks a sense of purpose set in. "I decided that it was up to me to do something about it," he remembers. Dennis plunged into the task of researching his own treatment and rapidly made some major changes in his life. He was a believer in alternative medicine and decided he did not want to take the traditional treatment of surgery and radiation. "I had read many books explaining the bad side effects," he said, and as a result embarked on his own healing program.

First he had all of his mercury amalgam fillings removed, then he did an eight-day fast and 90-day colon cleanse. He incorporated hydrology (water therapy), visualization and meditation into his life and changed his diet dramatically, eliminating all sugars, red meat, white flour, chocolate, vinegar, alcohol, black pepper and soft drinks. He switched to "reverse osmosis" water, drank plenty of fresh squeezed fruit and vegetable juices and started taking Essiac tea daily. He also did deep breathing exercises for 10 minutes twice a day and walked at least four kilometres a day, six days a week.

Although a CT scan in December indicated that his cancer had not spread, his PSA was up to 2.5 and his urologist made an appointment for him to see an oncologist. He was advised that the cancer had penetrated the capsule of the prostate and his condition was now even more serious. The oncologist suggested a six-month treatment of "Zoladex," a hormone designed to reduce levels of testosterone and shrink the tumour. This was to be followed by seven weeks of radiation. Although skeptical about the proposed treatment, Dennis was concerned by the latest news. He started taking the drug, but continued to seek complementary alternatives. In April he had his second shot of Zoladex and was given the encouraging news that his PSA was declining and the tumour was shrinking. Even so, Dennis was not convinced that this treatment was his best option.

That same month, Dennis learned about the opening of The Centre For Integrated Healing. He made an appointment and was impressed with his experience. "Every one was so helpful and friendly," he says, "It was like being at home." During his first appointment with the doctor he was complimented on his healing program. Dennis was the perfect example of someone who benefits from the Centre because he was not looking for directions, but rather to be empowered in his own choice of treatment. He was given information on a number of approaches using alternative medicine and was interested in an approach called "Cesium Therapy."

It was not an easy road, but the results were impressive. In June his PSA had dropped to .2 and Dennis passed his annual physical with flying colours. His confidence was so great that he refused radiation treatment. In September his PSA remained at .2 and Dennis requested another biopsy. In the euphoric days following his clear biopsy, Dennis believed his healing journey was complete and yet, in a way, it was only beginning.

Despite the good news he felt pressure building up inside him. He became extremely emotional and noticed a sense of anger and resentment welling up from deep inside. Describing himself as a pressure cooker with a stuck valve, the pressure had nowhere to go and Dennis finally exploded.

As a very private man, Dennis had not shared the details of his cancer with anyone outside of his immediate family. His wife of 49 years provided constant love and assistance according to Dennis. His two daughters, one of whom lives in North Vancouver and the other in Ireland, were also involved. Outside of his private family life, however, he had solely come to rely on the support of his wonderful doctor. The catalyst to his explosion was that his doctor, was leaving the Centre for Integrated Healing at the end of the year. Dennis found this impending change a devastating blow. "I had formed this powerful bond with her. I felt I was never going to see her again." Despite her assurances that he could see her in her private practice, Dennis could not take comfort in this possibility. He even felt abandoned as a result of her plans to take vacation over Christmas. Recognizing that Dennis needed some help, She suggested that he visit Hope House to see a counsellor. Hope House is a cancer centre where emotional, psychological and social support is offered to people with cancer. Kathy, his counsellor, was able to calm him down and encouraged him to start meditating again.

With the support of both Nancy and Kathy, Dennis started on the next part of his healing journey-his journey to wholeness. He discovered that he was carrying a lot of anger from his childhood. He had been sent to an English-style boarding school for boys on Vancouver Island. He had been angry about this and about the religion that had been forced upon him while there. Dennis became an atheist. During this healing time, however, in an opening experience that defies explanation, this all changed and Dennis discovered a spiritual person inside of him. Through this metamorphosis he was able to release his anger, and to forgive and love himself. "There is now a peace inside of me that never was there," he explains.

Dennis found himself drawn to books such as, "The Anatomy of the Soul," by Carolyn Myss and "Path with Heart," by Jack Kornfield. Gary Zukav's, "Seat of the

Soul," and "Soul Stories," are two others that continue to inspire him. Meditation has become a wonderful anchor for his spiritual practice and, to his own surprise, he finds himself praying on a regular basis. "I love to combine prayer with my walks through the natural beauty of the magnificent forests in Capilano Canyon." Dennis is a well-known volunteer, giving back to society by dedicating his time and energy to assist others who have cancer. He is truly a wonderful example of hope and empowerment to everyone he encounters.

"Curing my cancer was a walk in the park compared to the emotional aftermath." It was through contact with his emotions that his real healing occurred.

Dennis now sees his cancer as a gift because it has opened him up to a wonderful new world of spirit where he is finding new friends and allies on a journey that has never felt so good.

MORE DIETARY DETAIL...

Thoughts on food: Dennis loved to eat everything: steak, bacon, chocolate bars and especially desserts, which he ate daily at lunch and dinner. Now he chooses his food to nourish his body and soul, providing perfect and radiant health.

Top Five Dietary Changes:

- Eliminated dairy and coffee

- Eliminated all meats

- Stopped eating chocolate bars

- Learned new ways to bake with natural sweeteners and whole grain flours

- Always open to trying new recipes

No. 1 Recommendation: Eat a plant-foods (vegan) diet. Favourite cookbook: *Peaceful Palate* by Jennifer Raymond. Visit **www.stayingalivecoosbook.com/books**

Chapter Four:

Jack Fun's Story

Jack Fun's Story

On December 7th, 1998 a surgeon stapled up Jack Fun's chest and gave him a death sentence. "There's nothing that I can do; your tumour is too close to the aorta," he said. Later, at the Cancer Clinic, his oncologist was a little more specific, but no more optimistic. "You have a three per cent chance of lasting until year-end, but I would suggest you count on no more than three months," he advised. Jack sagged, weeping into the arms of his son, as the finality of the pronouncement struck him. Only three months to live!

I stared at the slim, healthy looking 65-year-old who sat opposite me, and who had obviously long outlived his diagnosis. "What happened?!" I asked him. He took me back to 1997 when he had developed a serious cough. At that time he was reassured by his physician that there was nothing to worry about and that it was probably a result of stress. One year later the cough remained a constant companion, however it had worsened to such an extent that Jack was afraid it may damage his chest. He sought a second opinion-one that sent him almost immediately to a surgeon who told him that there was a 14-centimeter growth on his lung. Jack was sent for tests and soon after was given the bad news. He had cancer and needed surgery immediately.

"The first word that came into my head was 'death'," he remembered, "and then I felt totally depressed and defeated." A friend of Jack's had mentioned a place called Hope House, which as its name implies, exists to give hope to people with cancer. Jack found his way there, where he learned that he could negotiate with the doctors and that he had rights as a patient. "I joined several support groups and I learned things such as stress reduction, self care and, unusual as it sounds, making friends with my disease," he said. He also learned that people in support groups live twice as long as people without that kind of support network. Jack received practical advice on how to make difficult decisions, such as whether or not he wanted to have chemotherapy, and was also re-introduced to meditation and visualization as tools to help overcome the disease. "I had learned to meditate a number of years ago to deal with stress, but my practice had become infrequent. It was a good reminder to start again. I certainly had all the motivation that I needed to keep up the discipline," he remembers.

Three months later, Jack was told by his oncologist that nothing more could be done for him except to delay the inevitable through chemotherapy and radiation treatment. It was then that Jack Fun's miraculous story took a turn. Within three minutes of his oncologist's ultimatum, something told Jack he was going to live. "I decided that I did not have to accept this," he told me. "At that moment my depression lifted and I was convinced I was better." No, he was not convinced that he could be better, but that he simply was better. Jack had five treatments of radiation, but did not like the way he felt. He declined chemotherapy and embarked on the next step of his positive healing.

While in the hospital he had been told about the Centre for Integrated Healing and made an appointment to see Dr. Hal Gunn. "Hal spent an hour and half with me," Jack said. "We talked a lot about the power of the mind to heal and that the first step is to have the will to live." Then Hal told Jack to start running again. "I was a bit taken aback," said Jack. "Here I was barely able to walk into the office and he is telling me to run again." But, Jack started to run and by May was running an hour-and-a-half a day. This was good for his cancer, but not so good for his 65-year-old knees, so he pared back to 50 miles a month. Hal explained later that he wanted Jack to focus on something that he associated with being well and running seemed to be the perfect thing.

Dr. Gunn also got Jack started on a program of supplements, vitamins and injections of MRV. (Mixed Respiratory Vaccine)

Jack made a number of additional changes in his life that he strongly believes contributed to his healing. He decided to reduce his stress by changing his job and he also eliminated people from his life who were a negative influence. He started to meditate every day and worked on visualizing himself in perfect health and indulging in all kinds of physical activities. Having already quit drinking alcohol, he went on to modify his diet; eliminating coffee, red meats and switching to more organic foods.

The result was the fit, active man I was interviewing about his story. "My tumour has reduced and Hal thinks it is now an immune mass, I have no pain or cough and I have gained 13 pounds," Jack said smiling. I wondered why Jack had been able to so effectively deny his prognosis and live while others go through denial but still die. Hal Gunn gave me his perspective: "I think that many people, when faced with death, deny it in their conscious mind, but underneath the surface they still think they will die.

Jack truly believes-at a deeper level-in the power of his mind to heal, and that makes all the difference.

When asked about the cause of his cancer, Jack confesses that he had always been "a stress freak," and thrived on it. "I had no idea that there could be consequences. I think my immune system always kept me out of trouble, but then I ran into a series of adversities." Jack was understating his adversities, as he'd been living through some very difficult times. He lost his life savings, had to move house, his relationship of the time fell apart and, if that was not enough, he had to take a job that he disliked to make ends meet. "I think my immune system couldn't cope anymore and I developed the disease from stress overload."

Jack concluded the interview with some profound comments about his experience. "It may seem strange to anyone looking in, but now I see there are benefits to this disease. My life has changed dramatically in the past months.

I take care of myself, I eat better, I meditate more often, my co-dependant behaviour has decreased. I live today as if it is my last and I plan like I will live forever. I know myself better. I am not my work or what I have accomplished or what I have accumulated. I've started to grow up."

I thanked him for sharing his journey with me and he smiled and told me that the most powerful shift he made had been to see his cancer as a gift. As I left, I thanked him for the gift of his story.

Chapter Five:

Robert Miller's Story

Robert Miller's Story

It is rare to hear that a diagnosis of cancer brought a sense of relief. However relief was Robert Miller's reaction when his doctor told him that he had follicular lymphoma. "In that moment, I knew I had no choice but to change my life," he said. His relief came despite the fact that, in the background, he heard the doctor's assistant exclaim, "That's incurable isn't it?"

In July of 1988 Robert was the dean of engineering technology programs at the Southern Alberta Institute of Technology, in Calgary. This had been his place of work for 22 years; half of these years as an instructor and the latter half as dean. He still kept his hand in teaching by instructing a wellness course and was, by all appearances, a befitting teacher. He was fit, active, a long distance runner and paid attention to his diet. He was not unduly alarmed when he felt a lump in the side of his neck while shaving one day. The locum general practitioner suggested observation until his own medical doctor returned from vacation. The second examination revealed another lump in his clavicle at the base of the neck. His doctor suggested a biopsy and this brought about his diagnosis of nodular lymphoma, as it was known at that time.

Nodular or follicular lymphoma is indeed incurable, therefore successful treatment means extending life expectancy as long as possible, which is normally eight to 10 years. The first step was the painful process of a bone marrow biopsy to assess how far the disease had progressed. Robert's results suggested that his cancer had reached stage four, the highest possible stage, where the cells were widely dispersed throughout the body. He was told that there were two options. The first involved an aggressive chemotherapy to try and knock out the cancer cells, while the second was simply to watch and wait. In view of the fact that Robert was exhibiting none of the common symptoms of the disease (these include night sweats, itching and weight loss) both he and his oncologist agreed that watchful waiting was the best strategy.

> *Robert knew his life was out of balance and he had been driving himself too hard in a job he did not enjoy.*

With a stressful job including the responsibility for 200 faculty members, the shared responsibility for three teenage daughters, a running regime of up to 60 miles a week, and trying to make do on five hours sleep a night, he had been burning the candle at both ends.

Robert knew he needed a dramatic change in his life. Through research, he confirmed that there was very little hope for an outright cure, and accepted that his challenge was to keep the cancer in check. He resigned from his job in 1991, taking early retirement at the age of 50. He decided he wanted to live in BC and chose Qualicum Beach on Vancouver Island as his new home. Putting his engineering and management background to work, he started to build custom houses. Although demanding, this new life had few of the intense political challenges of being a dean and he soon settled down to become a successful builder.

In 1994 he heard of Dr. Roger Rogers, the leading practitioner in the alternative treatment of cancer in the province at the time, and he made an appointment. As a patient who wanted to direct his own healing journey, Robert was delighted to find a doctor who supported him in treatments that he had researched himself. In fact, he believes

the support he received was critical to his well being.

While Robert was already following much of Dr. Rogers' advice, he became more convinced of certain dietary concerns and eliminated white sugar and white flour from his diet.

After eight years of remission, in 1988, he found himself sweating at night, suffering with bowel disorders and losing weight. His symptoms suggested the follicular cancer cells were transforming into a more aggressive form-a highly probable event in the course of this disorder. His doctor identified a major tumour in Robert's stomach and explained that the only treatment likely to help was a once-in-a-lifetime option due to the potential for heart damage. This option was a chemotherapy treatment comprised of four potent drugs. Robert says he felt like a pinch hitter going up for his one chance at bat.

Obviously he wanted to ensure this potent therapy had every opportunity to help him so he devised his own program to increase his chances of benefiting. "I wanted to encourage the chemo to get into every cell," he explained. After much research, his solution was hot baths and exercise. He would jog up the hill while waiting for the ferry at Horseshoe Bay-not an easy task when your red blood cells are depleted-and then would take an extremely hot bath when he got home. The chemotherapy was administered in six treatments, two weeks apart. It was a gruelling experience but it seemed to work and his doctor told him that he had responded dramatically well.

Another chapter of research and life changes began for Robert. "I had played a number of cards already," he said, "and now I had to be sure that I stayed healthy." His research, through a maze of scientific data, for a way to avoid another transformation resulted in a list of practical strategies. His diet changed once again. For example, he discovered that turmeric has beneficial effects and that omega-3 fatty acids, found in oil-rich fish such as wild Pacific salmon, could have a positive effect as well.

Robert prefers to obtain his nutrients through food rather than pills. Every morning he takes antioxidants in the form of blueberries and raspberries with his breakfast of organic brown rice, soymilk and turmeric. He has a mostly vegetarian diet supplemented with plenty of wild sockeye salmon. He takes hot baths to cleanse his inner body, since research suggests that this simulates a mild fever and heat-shock proteins, which is the body's natural reaction to infection. The result of this successful personal program resulted in a paper he wrote titled, "Strategies for Long Term Lymphoma Survival." He has broadened his contacts by developing his own lymphoma related website.

Today, as Robert outlives his diagnosed life expectancy, he says, "You wouldn't know I had anything wrong with me." He hikes in the mountains, cycles 12 miles many days of the year and sleeps at least seven hours a night. He attempts to live a balanced life and looks remarkably slim and fit for his 61 years of age. There is no doubt in Robert's mind, he says, that if you create a positive life with a strong will to live, a positive attitude will follow. He also has no doubt that the mind and body are entirely related.

A long way from the chaotic days in Calgary when he was first diagnosed with cancer, Robert now looks upon his diagnosis as being the necessary event "to knock me off my perch. I was unhappy but I didn't know how to change my life," he says. Robert's cancer has also brought meaning for the many other sufferers who have benefited from his insightful research and study of the subject. In addition to his report on survival strategies, he has written several other papers that are freely available from him by e-mail or through the website. Robert always believed that he could overcome his cancer. And now he is giving the gift of inspiration for survival to others.

MORE DIETARY DETAIL...

Old Favourites: Overall, Robert's diet didn't change a lot but he specifically avoids artificial sweeteners (aspartame) and partially hydrogenated fats, which are not always easy to identify.

Top Five Dietary Changes:

- Addition of turmeric to the diet

- No hydrogenated or partially hydrogenated fats

- No aspartame

- Foods with less (added) sugar

- More fish, specifically wild salmon from the North Pacific.

No. 1 Recommendation: Research your specific cancer and utilize evidence-based science to make medicinal food choices.

For some of Robert's research visit: **www.LymphomaSurvival.com**

Chapter Six:

Marie Pember's Story

Marie Pember's Story

Many years ago, Marie Pember had a vivid dream that she has always remembered. In this dream she placed her breast upon a guillotine blade to get rid of it. In May 2002 she discovered a lump on her breast and at first thought that it was just another of the many cysts that had plagued her all her adult life, but eventually suspected that her dream may be coming true.

Marie continued to find reasons to delay the inevitable check-up; a trip to Mexico and another to Montreal. Finally, when she figured it was time to deal with the situation. She went to her family doctor, who expressed some concern that she had left things so long. After the obligatory mammogram, followed by a sonogram and two biopsies (the first of which was negative) her suspicions were confirmed. It was cancer. A mastectomy was scheduled. Marie confessed to a certain amount of relief at losing her breast. "It had bothered me for a long time," she said, "and been a nuisance for many years."

Cancer had a formidable adversary in Marie, who admits that she did not pay much attention to what went into her body and frankly was far too busy to worry about a lump in her breast. Her life before her diagnosis was very full. As a competitive sales manager for Avon, Marie experienced significant stress. It was not unusual for her to cope with stress through a welcoming glass of wine when she got home from work. Outside of work her life was also very busy, with two grown sons and four grandsons who are very important to her.

While her friends expressed concern and sympathy, Marie actually felt a little bit of a fraud because she wasn't fearful in any way. Her faith in God was also helpful. "He doesn't bring me through anything that I cannot cope with," she explains. Her sons, Kevin and Tim, were "rocks of support." She sensed that as long as she didn't see fear in their eyes that she would be fine. In addition, her friends were very supportive. Joey, a dear companion and a nurse at the Vancouver Cancer clinic, took the time to go with Marie to each appointment with the oncologists, taking reams of notes and providing unbiased support. Another friend, Luena, accompanied her to the hospital before her surgery and gave her a Reiki treatment as she was being prepped and again in the recovery room. As Marie experienced a peace that pervaded her being, her friend smiled at her and commented, "You are simply taking this in your stride."

The surgery appeared to be routine and she checked out of the hospital after only one night. She took a couple of weeks off work but intended to return as soon as she could wear a bra. She retained her positive attitude explaining, "I don't have time for negativity," and looked forward to continuing her full life.

Her positive outlook received a jolt, however, when she was told that the cancer had spread to her lymph nodes. She needed further treatment. Her oncologist prescribed a course of chemotherapy followed by radiation and then hormone treatment. For a brief time Marie felt an unfamiliar sense of losing control and remembers thinking, "I wish someone would come in and make all these decisions." That's when she realized that it was time to take control and make decisions that felt right to her. "That was when it became my journey," she explains.

The first thing she did was make an appointment with her oncologist to ask some questions about her treatment. He dismissed her diet concerns explaining, "In my profession I see no evidence of a connection between diet and cancer." Then, when she expressed concerns about the chemotherapy eliminating her immune system, he ushered her out of his office with the condescending assurance that she should not worry and that he would take good care of her. This was accompanied by a conciliatory kiss on the cheek. Marie was less than impressed or reassured.

Her personal healing journey continued with a visit to a naturopath who referred her to the Centre for Integrated Healing. As the Centre's two-day introductory program coincided with her chemotherapy appointment, she postponed the treatment. With her daughter-in-law Kathy as her "support person," Marie attended the program and describes it as two wonderfully peaceful days with an overwhelming feeling of joy. She says everything she heard made sense to her.

Exploring a more natural way of healing and building her immune system seemed to be the path she had been seeking.

When she reviewed the pros and cons of having chemotherapy, she knew that this was not a road she could take. "I could not take something that would wipe out my immune system at the time that I needed it most," she says.

Marie made the most of the facilities offered at the Centre, meeting with Dr Anita Tannis, Sally Errey the nutritionist and Lisa Solanto, who helped her with visualization and meditation. As a result of this informative part of her journey, Marie realized she needed to make substantial changes in her life. And although she knew that God was with her all the time, she also knew it was time to create more room for Him. Her contact with Sally Errey made an enormous impact on her life and health. "Sally helped me understand the definition of insanity. I could not do the same things over and over and expect different results," she shares.

"Sally set me on a path to a different way to eat."

The result was a dramatic shift in her diet, although Marie prefers not to use the term "diet." "This was about changing eating habits," she says. She eliminated dairy and refined sugar from her menu, reduced her intake of fat, stopped eating red meat, and switched from black tea and coffee to green tea. She started to consume more fresh salad and vegetables and even gave up red wine. Marie also started some supplements, including garlic and Floressence tea, to boost her immune system.

When it was time to visit an oncologist again, he was delighted to see what good health she was in and recommended a stronger drug that could be administered for a longer period. She felt convinced that this was not the right course of treatment for her, but did not want to finalize her decision without consulting her "board of directors," her sons. After she had explained the treatment and the potential side effects that could affect the quality of her life for such a lengthy period of time, her eldest son asked her, "Haven't you got better things to do for the next two years?" She advised the doctor of her decision and in a decidedly uncompromising manner he told her that when it comes back it would be even harder for him to get. He referred her to a radiation oncologist who reviewed the benefits of radiation designed to kill residual cancer cells with relatively fewer side effects. Marie agreed to this treatment feeling that it was the middle road.

With her characteristic positive attitude she turned the 20-day treatment plan into a positive healing environment. First she re-named the treatment chamber "the healing room," then she created a visualization that maximized the benefits of the radiation while eliminating fear and anxiety. She asked the attendants to play soft classical music and she surrounded the bed with images of those she loved.

Seeing Marie, an elegant, articulate, attractive woman who looks far younger than her 64 years, I would never guess that she had been diagnosed with cancer less than a year ago. She is a remarkable person who is able to see a gift in her cancer. She realizes that cancer has helped her improve the quality of her life and her health. She has moved from what she describes as a "much darker space," into a lighter way of dealing with life. Wayne Dyer, in his book "Your Sacred Self," presented her with the secret to managing stress. His words "You can choose peace," resonated with Marie and now she tries to seek the peaceful way when confronted with life's challenges, realizing she can choose not to get angry or stressed. And, instead of working so much, Marie has realized how important it is to give back to society. After years of procrastination, she now volunteers and has discovered the truth of the statement, "The more love you give, the more you receive."

MORE DIETARY DETAIL...

Old Favourites: Marie realized her work took over her life and she relied on a couple of glasses of wine each night to wind down. Favourite foods were anything that could be got easily to the table, such as frozen meats, entrees and vegetables, with little consideration for content.

No. 1 Recommendation: Stop, look and listen!

- **Stop** – take the time to assess what you have been eating; it may be contributing to a suppressed immune system and allow cancer to happen.

- **Look** – at what you eat and ask yourself "is this going to profit or pollute my body?"

- **Listen** – to a nutritionist who really understands the role of diet in cancer prevention, and most importantly in re-building your immune system to optimum health.

Chapter Seven:

Brad Funk's Story

Brad Funk's Story

Brad's story is one that has the making of a great drama...and one with the potential for tragedy. It all started back in 1994 when Brad saw an opportunity to combine his interest in preserving the environment with an opportunity to earn a living. He had just moved to Vancouver Island when he learned about the business of taking houses that were slated for demolition in Vancouver and relocating them to the Island. He loved the idea of rescuing a dwelling from destruction and preserving it for a new owner. He joined a company to sell the homes that they saved. He felt inspired and over a four year period sold, moved and saved 45 houses from becoming landfill.

His comfortable world, however, was itself demolished in July of 1997, when one of the owners of the company quietly declared personal bankruptcy. Brad felt terrible. He had been persuading customers to part with up to 50 percent of the purchase price on homes yet to be delivered, and now this money had disappeared. Personally, most of his own savings were tied up in monies the company owed him and three houses that he had moved. The house in which he and his fiancée were living had been completed and resold, they were to move into the second after their upcoming marriage, and the third, their future home, was yet uninhabitable requiring extensive renovations. This, in itself, would have been a sad enough story. But it was only the beginning of a living nightmare leading to illness for Brad.

One of the couples who had lost their life savings in their investment for a home, retained a lawyer and received significant coverage on local TV. An RCMP investigation was launched and Brad worked closely with the police to provide information. Brad suspected that he could not retrieve any of the money owed to his previous clients or the significant sum owed to himself, but was committed to seeing justice prevail; little realizing the turmoil this would create in his own life. In the following months Brad's stress levels reached stratospheric heights. The twisted story in which he found himself included destruction, deceit, vandalism, financial ruin and even a law suit filed against him on the way to his wedding.

Brad knew he was going to get cancer. When mild symptoms of lassitude and fatigue developed his doctor told him not to worry, insisting he was just a little anemic. But Brad was not convinced and pushed his doctor for more blood tests. A specialist at St. Paul's Hospital suggested a very specialized test where each individual cell was analyzed. But before the test results were in, Brad was on his way to sea for 28 days. He had started to work with the Canadian Coast Guard to help meet expenses. He spent all of his spare time repairing his house, which had been vandalized, so his wife and family could join him, dealing with the bank that illegally froze his monies through a frivolous and vexatious lawsuit launched by his former employer, and working with the RCMP to secure convictions.

The ship he was on was about 500 miles off the West Coast when he received an e-mail saying the doctor's office wanted to see him immediately. He called and tried to explain his work situation, but found the doctor very insistent. Brad's fear intensified when the captain, who stepped in and spoke with the doctor, gave the order to abandon the major science program that they were conducting and head back to port. It was at St. Joseph's Hospital in Comox that a bone marrow test confirmed that Brad had an extremely rare form of cancer called Hairy Cell Leukemia.

Brad was advised that the treatment was chemotherapy and that his life expectancy was five years. Naturally he was devastated and filled with sadness about the life he was going to miss with his new family. Fortuitously, a friend of his forwarded a copy of a local magazine that featured an article about the healing journey of Dennis Thulin, a cancer patient at the Centre for Integrated Healing in Vancouver. Brad made an appointment to attend the next Introductory Program at the Centre.

It was during this time that he believes his life changed. Dr. Hal Gunn, co-director and resident physician at the Centre, encouraged Brad to share the story of the events preceding his diagnosis. When he finished, Brad remembers Hal asking him a simple question: "What is really important to you?" In that moment, Brad knew that what mattered most was his recovery and that regaining his health would require him to drop all the activities causing him so much stress. "They just weren't worth dying for," he said.

The information and support Brad obtained from the Centre continued to impact his life. He improved his diet, buying only organic vegetables, cutting down on red meat and switching to soymilk and brown rice, for instance. He started to meditate, took the recommended vitamins and supplements and attended weekly Healing Touch and relaxation sessions. He worked on relaxing more and refocusing his life on what was positive. While it was not easy to let go of the problems and drama that had dominated his life for so long, he knew how important it was for his health. Thanks to the expertise and confidence of his doctor at St. Paul's Hospital, his week undergoing chemotherapy was inspiring, though difficult.

In January of 2002, four and a half years after the life he'd built in the housing market crumbled, Brad sensed he was going to get well.

"Everything was working together-my diet, the healing touch, my spiritual work-and I just knew I was going to be okay."

By April the same year, Brad's blood test showed that he was completely clear of the cancer. It was a moment of great jubilation, combined with quiet reflection. He was happy about the positive results, but Brad had a feeling that the immense stress he had been under had caused his immune system to stop coping.

He had created his disease.

Instead of a tragic ending to his story, Brad's life has changed in many profound ways since developing cancer. He now recognizes the power of one's mind to dramatically influence one's health. He has a new sense of spiritual connection, and says, "I never believed in God, but now I know there is something that connects us all together." He has become a boat builder, fulfilling a dream that has filled his heart for years. He knows that cancer saved his life. "I was spiraling downward," he confesses. "Now I like myself, I am closer to my family and I am going to be well."

For an even happier ending, he and his wife Lenore received the gift of a second child, Annika Kathleen Funk, in February 2003. What a lovely postscript to an inspiring story!

MORE DIETARY DETAIL...

Old Favourites: A self professed "starch hound," Brad's favourite foods were French fries, potato chips, breads and crackers.

Top Five Dietary Changes:

- Now eats organic produce

- Cut out fast foods

- Incorporated whole grains and natural sweeteners

- Rarely eats meat

- Eats at home more frequently

No. 1 Recommendation: Source organic produce and understand the need for complex carbohydrates and their sources.

Check out: **www.stayingalivecookbook.com/links**

Chapter Eight:

Signy Wilson's Story

Signy Wilson's Story

You get some idea of who Signy Wilson is from her voice mail message: "The greater the obstacle, the more the glory in overcoming it." A 33-year-old self-proclaimed extrovert, Signy is both energetic and articulate. She is also very intuitive and despite having no family history of breast cancer, had always known something could occur. Her first sign of a problem was discovered during a phone call when her arm brushed a noticeable lump in her breast.

Her immediate reaction was panic and tears, yet in the midst of her turmoil she heard a quiet inner voice say: "You don't have to worry about this, my dear." Intensely spiritual, Signy and her sense of the divine feminine, or "The Goddess," as she says, has been a profound source of comfort and guidance. She immediately felt much calmer and was convinced that this was not cancer. However, after a period of tests and waiting, she was dismayed to find out that, indeed, it was.

Suddenly, Signy found herself swept up into the arena of conventional cancer care. She was introduced to her surgeon, who she found patronizing, disrespectful and condescending, and was told that they must first check for any signs that cancer had spread. The prognosis was good and the surgeon proposed a lumpectomy together with the removal of some lymph nodes. Somewhat reluctantly, Signy was scheduled for surgery. "I was caught up in the panic and sense of urgency" she says, "so I kept over-riding my inner voice." When she was able to calm herself Signy found her inner guide was clearly telling her to slow down. "My body, mind and spirit were not aligned," she explains, and "I knew I could not entrust my sacred temple to this surgeon." She postponed the surgery. Needing the support of her closest friends, Signy formed "Team Signy," a group of women who were dedicated to assisting her on this journey back to health. The result was overwhelming, and she felt the euphoria of being loved and prayed for. "Every minute of every day someone will be thinking about you," she was told. Her surgery was rescheduled for May 9th. She felt she should cancel, but was held back by the fear that she may not find an alternative surgeon. It was about this time she heard about the Centre for Integrated Healing-a divine synchronicity that helped her resolve her dilemma. The next Introductory Program at the Centre was scheduled for the same day as her surgery. "I knew what my heart was telling me to do," she recalls. "I called the surgeon and cancelled."

Her visit to the Centre for Integrated Healing was not revolutionary since she already practiced many of the foundations of healing they introduced. She believed in the integration of body, mind and spirit in healing. Her diet was good. She drank no alcohol or coffee, ate little meat and her only bad habits were cheese and sugar. Yet she enjoyed the atmosphere of healing and love, and also found her visit to the Centre very affirming. Sally Errey helped her to understand the sound principles behind her diet, and Dr. Anita Tannis helped her feel empowered to make her own healing choices. She started on the vitamin and supplement program and began taking control of her healing journey. After finding a surgeon she trusted, her operation was scheduled for May 16th., which was perfect for Signy who was resolved to participate in a leadership program in California on May 29th.

Signy's commitment to personal empowerment meant putting her own imprint on her hospital stay. She had her own food brought in, including organic carrot juice and was inspired by a personal selection of music. Her friends were constantly encouraging her through prayer and affirmations and prior to her surgery she created a ritual image to help her. "I am the sacred daughter of the Goddess, you are the high priestess," she told her surgeon. "The operating table is the altar and the hospital is the temple." With this inspiring image it is no surprise that Signy came through the operation successfully and recuperated in time to go to California less than two weeks later.

One may have expected that her retreat would provide plenty of opportunity for rest and relaxation after the ordeal of surgery. However this was not Signy's way at all. This retreat involved tests of strength and confidence that would challenge anyone, let alone someone who had recently vacated a hospital bed. When questioned by others about her obsession to complete these demanding physical challenges, she praised the support and encouragement of her instructors. "They told me that breast cancer survivors who undergo this training are less likely to have a relapse. In addition she found a special gift, which reframed her vision of the future. "I was resigning myself to living life on the fringe. I had trouble visualizing myself in a relationship, having children or even working." All this changed during her profound experience as she came to trust her body again. "I knew it would go the distance for me. I could participate fully in life again."

Signy's euphoria received a setback when she returned to Vancouver and was told that she needed to have chemotherapy. Somehow this possibility had escaped her as she had assumed that her treatment was over.

> **It is unlikely that the Cancer Agency had experienced chemotherapy becoming a "sacred ritual" before.**

Signy's room was decorated with Goddess icons, prayers were said before the procedure started and the red chemothapy fluid became "an elixir of the Goddess."

It was now time to face one of the more challenging side effects, which was the loss of her hair. Signy is a Leo and described her hair as a mane. She was unwilling to sit by and watch her hair fall out so Team Signy conducted an elaborate ritual to claim the power of her hair by ceremonially removing it. "They adorned me, did my nails and make up and then I observed my hair one last time in a mirror that my grandmother had given me." In a series of steps, her luxuriant tresses were removed with Signy performing the final ritualistic shave herself. "It was both scary and profound," she remembers. "I was not sure who I had become."

Signy has had a number of scares since her treatment finished however her doctors have been affirming that there is no abnormality in her healing. She feels that her cancer has been a divine wake-up call. She knows she has been journeying to rediscover her authenticity. She needed to live her own life and not try to be someone else. "God made me how I am. She made me this way for a very special reason," she says. Facing up to the powerful people who, at times, have tried to take over her treatment resulted in her own empowerment. She has learned how to ask for help and in return her friends have benefited as well. She has experienced the power of prayer and love. And she believes she is much softer, gentler and more compassionate with herself and others, while still being able to enforce her boundaries.

Signy says she feels her relationship with the Goddess guided her healing journey, and that this experience is but part of a greater journey towards wholeness. She is living proof, as her telephone message says, that "The greater the obstacle, the more the glory in overcoming it."

MORE DIETARY DETAIL...

Old Favourites: To Signy, food was about re-fuelling and anything would do – cheese and crackers and grilled cheese sandwiches were standbys. Ice-cream and pastries were her favourite foods.

Top Five Dietary Changes:

- Vegetable juice every day

- "Power smoothies" and oatmeal

- Cleaned out cupboards – threw away anything refined, processed, with sugar or hydrogenated fats

- Eliminated dairy, sugar and chicken

- Used food and herbs as medicine (e.g. burdock, nettles and dandelion).

No. 1 Recommendation: Be gentle with yourself and take the time to adjust.

Check out: Susun Weed,s "Breast cancer? Breast health! The Wise Woman Way" and the Green Door Restaurant Vegetarian Cookbook by Poppy Weaver and Ron Farmer at www.stayingalivecookbook.com/books

Chapter Nine:

Mel Lehan's Story

Mel Lehan's Story

Mel Lehan never got ill. He followed all the recommendations for a healthy diet. He did not drink coffee, ate no salt or sugar and was a vegetarian. He ran 30 kilometres a week and had even completed a half marathon. "I was a poster boy for good health" he says. That's not all; he was happy, too. He loved his wife and three daughters and was doing exactly what he wanted to do with his life.

So how did he end up with cancer? After a 20-year teaching career, Mel decided to take on the role of caregiver for his third child and enjoyed every minute of it. "I got to stay at home and spend time on what I love-my children and the community around me." It was doing what he loved, in part, however, that resulted in too little time for himself and too much stress-even if it was for a good cause.

A dedicated activist, Mel's five-year battle against City Hall to preserve the Kitsilano neighbourhood from developers was one of his many causes. According to Mel, Kitsilano was changing as developers eliminated affordable housing and built high-end condos. He devoted himself to stopping them and personally organized a block representation system. He proudly remembers his successful efforts to get from 800 to 1,000 people out to every meeting until City Hall finally gave in. "They never had a battle like this in their history," Mel suggests, "It was tremendously satisfying and I just loved it."

Mel, a slim wiry figure, who barely contains his own intense energy, thrived on the community involvement and went on to dedicate himself and his talents to many other challenges. Until one day he felt a bit of discomfort when he swallowed. Mel was not concerned, however as a precaution decided to see his GP who proposed a barium test. His peace of mind, and life as he knew it, was shattered when his doctor called. "We have discovered a lump on your esophagus and are pretty sure it's cancerous," she stated. Mel was deeply shocked, having believed that, somehow, only other people got cancer. Surely, it was not something that could happen to someone like him. But here it was happening.

Mel's organizer's mind went to work. He called his doctor back and suggested that as they suspected the worst, he wanted to schedule the next set of tests. By the end of the day his CAT scan and biopsy were arranged. By the week's end he was told he had a very large tumour in his esophagus and that it was malignant. There was an 85 per cent chance he would die within five years.

His operation was scheduled for the following Monday, only 12 days after diagnosis. "I could not believe how fast my life had been turned around." The week leading up to his surgery was a whirlwind of activity. It was expected he would survive the four hour operation, but Mel wasn't taking any chances. There were no doubts about what he had to do. He quit his work responsibilities and spent some time putting his financial affairs in order. Then he went to Seattle to catch a game of his "beloved baseball" prior to the most difficult task of all-telling his children the news. "Being told I had cancer was nothing compared to this," he recalls. He tried to make light of it, but the seriousness of the situation was not lost on his children. On the day before Mel entered hospital he and his family went for what could be their last picnic.

The reality of his cancer became all too real once he arrived at the hospital and was handed a razor with which to shave the body hair from his throat to his navel. "Until that moment I thought the whole experience might just go away. Now I realized that there was no escape." The operation would result in the removal of his esophagus and the attachment of his stomach to the neck. He survived the operation and received good news and bad news as a result. The good news was that the operation had been successful in removing all the active cancer. However, the cancer had metastacized and Mel now only had a 15 per cent chance of outliving his condition.

It was at this point that Mel says he decided that he may as well be one of the 15 per cent. He commenced his personal healing journey immediately. Although this marathon runner could hardly move, he asked if he could go for a walk. He made for a strange figure, connected by a multiplicity of tubes to his walker, but walk he did. He struggled for only three minutes but made a personal commitment that he would walk for at least five minutes every hour. He believed that physical fitness was going to be the key to his survival. After ten days he was released from hospital and engaged in a vigorous walking program of four kilometres, three times a day-84 kilometres a week.

It was about this time that, at the suggestion of three different friends, he visited Dr. Rogers at the Centre for Integrated Healing. Mel's practical mindset appreciated the nature of the alternatives that he had to consider and liked being empowered to make his own decisions.

> *He switched to organic fruit and vegetables, started a regime of vitamins and supplements and began taking Floressence.*

In addition, he chose to have MRV (Mixed Respiratory Vaccine) injections to boost his immune system and decided to proceed with chemotherapy. After five treatments of chemo, however, Mel's body could not take any more so he terminated this therapy.

Meanwhile, throughout his healing program, Mel started to appreciate the positive things happening as a result of his cancer. He received astonishing love and support from his friends and his community. He also spent time contemplating the possible connection between his cancer and his lifestyle. He realized that although he had been enjoying his life it was stressful and imbalanced. He had been taking very little time for his own personal needs-instead focusing only on his family and community. With this realization,

> *he gave himself permission to do things he enjoyed, such as being in nature and riding his bike.*

He began to make the most of his life in a balanced way. He took his youngest daughter to Disneyland, and the older two girls for a wonderful week in New York.

Then he took himself to baseball spring training to watch his favourite team, the Milwaukee Brewers . A friend of his managed to arrange a visit with Mel's hero, Cal Ripkin. They chatted for about 20 minutes and then, to Mel's delight, Cal agreed to play catch. It was "a pinnacle moment of my life," he says. Two friends arranged benefits for Mel and raised $20,000, which paid for a five-week family trip to Europe.

One year later, Mel's survival chances improved to 50 per cent. After two years his likelihood of survival was 80 per cent. Today, more than three years later, Mel's future looks positive. He believes a combination of factors contributed to his successful healing, including his positive attitude, good physical condition, eating a good diet, reducing his stress, enjoying restful sleep, the immune boosters, his loving family and friends and, most importantly, luck. Luck? It seems Mel Lehan is a living example of creating one's own luck.

MORE DIETARY DETAIL...

Thoughts on food: Mel was fairly health orientated but generally "ate to live," rather than for the love of food. Now he enjoys his food, grazes continually and finds food so much more fun.

Top Five Dietary Changes:

• Eats more frequently (due to "new plumbing")

• Eats organic

• Eats more fruit and vegetables

• Reduced toxicity and exposure to chemicals

• Has fun with food

No. 1 Recommendation: Eat whole and organic foods as much as possible. Eat slowly to aid digestion.

Visit **www.acor.org** for online cancer resources.

Chapter Ten:

The Cancer Conqueror's Kitchen

The Cancer Conqueror's Kitchen

As you commit to giving yourself only the very best care, you will spend more time preparing food. How you feel about this will depend on your previous relationship with the kitchen! Maybe you grew up in an environment where your mother or grandmother created comfort food made with love and devotion for their families. Or was your food prepared in a forced rush, looked upon as another chore to be completed before getting on to the next household task?

Taking the time to personalize and fine-tune your kitchen can transform it into a pleasant place to be, where peaceful moments can be found along with gratitude for the abundance of foods brought to us.

Fortunately, the modern kitchen saves valuable time. Working in a well organized, efficient kitchen can make all the difference in how quickly a meal can be put together.

Kitchen Environment

Have a good look around your kitchen. Do you like the colour of the walls? Is there cluttering that is irritating you? Can your kitchen be improved by plants? All these elements can play a huge part in enhancing (or detracting from) your kitchen experience.

Here are some simple and easy suggestions that don't require a full kitchen overhaul:

• Add photos of family, friends or happy vacation shots.

• Add plants. If there is no sunlight, consider artificial green plants and decorative fruits and vegetables – they will have the same effect.

• Reduce clutter by placing smaller items in decorative boxes or remove non-essentials from the kitchen.

• Add a quote to inspire a smile. One of my personal favourites is: "Cooking is like Love. It should be entered into with care-free abandon or not at all," and "Never trust a skinny cook," always gets a laugh.

• Organize here, organize there, organize everywhere!

Organizing your Kitchen

This is best done by spending some time outside of the kitchen and assessing the main activities you do while you're in there. Jot down any points that are irritating or awkward.

Gather together all the items you use DAILY. Weed out the smaller, handy items that are only used occasionally.

Start with cooking utensils, then do bowls and pots and pans. Most people use a fry pan and the same two pots repeatedly.

Place all the daily utensils in a wide-mouthed jar on the counter top, you will need easy access to them. Place the other utensils in a near-by drawer.
Place the regularly used bowls and pots in the cupboards close to the oven burners. Put all the other items in the back of the cupboards. Often all the pots and pans are put together, but the goal of this new organization is to put all the frequently used items together, for easy access.

Allow room for electrical appliances. Depending on your setup, you can have them on the counter, or in a hutch. Sometimes a free standing shelving unit can be the perfect solution for storing appliances. If it is sturdy enough, you can use the appliances right from the shelf, rather than move them to the counter and back. Organize your spices into the 10 most commonly used. These usually include: basil, cumin, Italian herbs, curry powder, parsley, cinnamon, oregano and chili flakes. This is a worthwhile rainy day project. Use large labels to clearly identify them and have them readily accessible.

Old spices can become rancid and lose their taste. Throw out any old, not recently used spices, and buy spices as you need them, in small (one to four tablespoons) quantities.

Re-group and label the rest of the spices and store them in a drawer or cupboard. Small plastic baskets are an excellent way to store many small jars. The basket can simply be pulled out and placed on the counter while you search for a spice, which is much quicker than lifting and looking behind every jar with your head in the cupboard. Or, of course, you can invest in a spice rack.

Have your kitchen and paper towels in a nearby spot to quickly clean up any spills (without creating further mess).

Now that your work space is organized and uncluttered, it's time to look at the essential equipment you'll need for a pleasant and speedy kitchen experience.

Non-Electrical Equipment

Sharp Chopping Knife
It's time to put away those old bent steak knives you've been trying to chop your veggies with. A well-designed, high quality chopping knife is one of the best investments you'll make and it will have you feeling like a chef in no time. Test an 8 or 10-inch knife at your local kitchen store. Make sure there is good clearance between your knuckles and the chopping board. Buy in the medium to high price range, you won't regret it, but you will regret having to work with a cheap knife that doesn't do the work for you.

Baker's Scraper
A new addition to the kitchen, this handy tool helps scrape up chopped items from the chopping board and transfer them into the pot with minimum mess. If

you have small hands you will have experienced trying to scoop up chopped tomato pieces, only to have some of them slip out of your hands and splatter on the counter top. This simple tool can really add speed to putting recipes together and makes clean up easier.

Paring Knife

A paring knife is ideal for smaller jobs and for working with soft and frozen fruits and tomatoes. Keep all knives sharp and avoid using them as screwdrivers and tin openers! This one simple rule will keep them useful longer!

Chopping Board, Small and Large

Wooden chopping boards have a certain aesthetic appeal and are easy to clean with lemon juice and baking soda. Buy a board at least one inch thick and store flat to reduce warping.

Plastic boards are lighter, easy to store and can be cleaned the same way as wooden boards, or wash well in a dishwasher.

Garlic Press

A well-designed garlic press will help add flavour to your recipes and the crushing allows for more nutritious phytochemicals to be released. The press is best used for when two or more cloves of garlic are called for. You may be able to chop two cloves of garlic quicker than it would take to press them and then wash the press. Leave the press to soak in water if you don't get to washing it immediately. The small dried garlic pieces are very difficult to remove.

Vegetable Peeler

A large percentage of the vitamins and carotenes (coloured pigments proven to prevent disease) are found in the skins of fruits and vegetables, so you won't need to use this very often. However, sometimes you'll need to peel a yam or potato and it's well worth having a good peeler on hand to at least make the experience more enjoyable – and so that the vegetables, not your fingers, end up skinless.

Wire Mesh Strainer

Buy a large wire stainless steel mesh strainer for rinsing grains and beans before cooking and also for rinsing grains after cooking. Rinsing helps remove some of the glutinous soluble fibre thus retaining the fluffy nature of the grain. Rinsed grains can then be stored and used for grain salads (see recipes section). Keep your strainer dry after use to prevent rust spots.

Colander

Another handy item, the colander can be used as a container when washing fruits and vegetables, as well as a bowl for storing those fresh washed veggies before they get prepared for the recipe. If the holes are small enough, the colander can also be used to rinse some of the larger grains such as brown rice, barley and wheat berries.

Pyrex Glass Measuring Cups

For pouring liquids and pre-mixing stock and sauces, have a selection of one, two and four cup versions.

Kitchen Timer

Having this gadget saves watching the clock and can make the difference between a delicious meal or a disaster. Have two in your kitchen.

Miscellaneous

You'll also need wooden spoons, measuring cups, measuring spoons and spatulas.

Pots

Two-Quart Sauce Pan

For making sauces, oatmeal and sautéing small amounts of garlic, onions or mushrooms, this pot is perfect.

Eight-Quart Stockpot

Just right for making soups and stews and having room to double the recipe so you can freeze half for future meals.

Electrical Appliances

Skillet

An electric skillet or "Dutch Oven" can be quite versatile and used as both a fry pan and a skillet for cooking chilies, curries and pasta sauces. Look for a non-stick variety and make sure you use non-scratch utensils with it. Once the surface is extensively scratched an acidic sauce, such as tomato sauce, can leach some of the metals from the skillet into your food. If this has happened, it's time to replace the skillet.

Food Processor, with Slicing and Grating Blade

The most important help you'll have in the kitchen, is from the processor. Chopping vegetables for soups and chilies can literally take hours for some people (especially with a steak knife and a warped chopping board!)
A food processor with a chopping, slicing and grating blade means dinner can be served within the hour. For a soup, almost everything can go through the processor and then tossed into the pot – onions, garlic, carrots, celery, potatoes, yams, mushrooms etc. The processor does them uniformly so that, after cooking, the vegetables are all soft at the same time. I cannot emphasize enough how dramatic a difference the food processor makes. I've prepared soups for crock-pot cooking in as little as 12 minutes. Test a model before buying. Look for a quiet motor, ease of putting together, safety features and ease of cleaning.

Hand Blender

A hand blender is perfect for making smoothies, quick bean dips and to blend soups in the pot (often giving them a creamier, more gourmet appeal). The hand blender is much easier to clean than your processor and/or blender and this is why I recommend it. Good models are readily available and affordable. Hand blending soups after cooking results in a wonderful texture and is perfect for soups such as cream of carrot or tomato. As well, when planning to blend, the food processor can be used when making soup since the vegetables don't have to be cut specific sizes. A hand blender also saves the inconvenience of transferring hot soups into blenders to be blended in batches.

Blender

A food processor and a hand blender will probably satisfy your needs, but a stand alone blender can be useful for doing most of the things a food processor can do- chop nuts, make smoothies, blend sauces and soups. Blenders don't get sauces as smooth as a processor but 90 per cent of the time you'll get the results you need. Look for a blender with chop, purée and blend options. These options are variations on machine speed. Test a model before buying. Look for a quiet motor, ease of putting together, safety features and ease of cleaning.

Juicer

Juicing can be an easy affordable way to maximize your vitamin, mineral, enzyme and phytochemical intake. Juicing regularly is an investment in your daily and future health and will ultimately save you money on supplements.

If you are considering buying a new juicer, be reminded that you really do get what you pay for. Low priced juicers have a reputation for not lasting more than a year. Mid to high priced juicers come with a 10-25 year warranty (one of the few appliances left in the marketplace that do!) on their engines. Most juicers remove the indigestible plant fibres and retain the water and nutrient content. Other "juice" machines, retain the fibre and can make soups and a variety of other things. These machines fall in the higher price category but can be a good investment if used regularly.

Juicing can play a part of a healthful, whole foods diet that is already high in fibre, as long as it does not replace fresh vegetable intake. Most beneficial is a juice made from a variety of vegetables including something green.

You may be able to find a juicer second-hand at a yard sale or advertised in the classifieds. Many people go on a "health-kick," and then find daily juicing too inconvenient. (Juicers do take time to assemble, clean and re-assemble.) Ask around, you may be able to borrow one from a friend or family member. Don't be put off if the juicer is stained. It doesn't mean the former owner didn't clean and look after it. I brought home my beautiful white juicer and it was irreversibly stained after the first carrot juice!

Chapter Eleven:

Buying Organic

Buying Organic

Now that you've set up a sacred space for healing in the kitchen, it's time to fill it with health promoting and cancer-fighting foods. An understanding of where our food is coming from can make the "what, how, when and where" of food shopping much simpler.

Our food comes from a variety of sources outside of our homes. In the last 50 years, we have handed our food production over to others. The integrity and judgment we would personally use in growing our own foods is not always guaranteed. Commercial crops are being grown using the "agribusiness" model of mono-cropping, with extensive artificial fertilizer and intensive agricultural chemical usage.

You may have noticed some new sections in your supermarket - an "Organic Produce" island, or some organic cereals, tomato sauces, pastas and beans in the health food section. These new options are a reflection of the growing trend towards organic foods.

What is organic?

While organic is the new buzz word in health circles, it's not a passing fad. It is simply a resurrection of ancient farming practices. Certified organic foods and products are derived from a natural system that excludes the use of synthetically compounded fertilizers, pesticides, growth regulators and livestock feed additives such as antibiotics. In addition, organic agriculture defined by the North American organic standards, prohibits the use of genetically engineered modifications, sewage sludge as a soil additive, or ionizing radiation as a food preservation technique. The primary purpose of organic farming is to provide healthy food with practices that are sustainable, so that future generations will be able to continue to benefit from well nourished soil.

Why has organic become so important?

There are many factors that encourage people to produce and consume more organic foods. These generally are improved health, reduced environmental impact and ethical considerations.

Organic food has no pesticides

Pesticides have been linked to breast cancer, prostate cancer and non-Hodgkin's lymphoma, as well as male and female infertility and birth defects. An estimated 90 per cent of fungicides cause cancer in experimental animals. More than 200,000 people worldwide die each year from pesticide poisoning. Continued low-level exposure to pesticides has been correlated with headaches, dizziness, nausea, vomiting and mental confusion.

Protect our children

Children have a higher percentage of body fat per total body weight when compared with adults. Since pesticides are often stored in the fatty tissues, children are especially susceptible to pesticides. An estimated 25 per cent of the currently used pesticides enter both plants and animals and cannot be easily removed. Research by the National Cancer Institute (USA) reports that children are up to six times more likely to develop childhood leukemia when pesticides are used in the home and garden. A study in the American Journal of Public Health (1995) found increased incidence of cancer in children from homes where pesticides were used in the yard.

Bioaccumulation

Pesticide and toxin residue is exacerbated as we move up the food chain. Plant foods are far less toxic due to their low fat content. As animals eat the corn, soy, grains and rendered animal products that they are fed, any toxins get stored and accumulated in the fatty tissues. Humans are at the top of this food chain and are therefore exposed to accumulated toxins every day from animal's milk, yogurt, cheese, egg, meat and fish consumption. If you continue to eat animal foods, make sure they are organic or appropriately raised.

Organic foods have no endocrine-disrupting chemicals

Many pesticides currently used by agri-business are endocrine-disrupters. These artificial chemicals interfere with our hormones that regulate reproduction, growth, and mental and physical development. University of Wisconsin researchers found that pesticide exposure damaged the nervous system, immune and endocrine (hormone) systems of animals and increased the incidence of aggression.

Organic is non-irradiated food

You may not know it, but many foods are irradiated, using enormous levels of radiation emitted by radioactive isotopes, to increase shelf life. To delay fruit ripening, a level equivalent of 50,000 X-rays is used. To kill insects and bacterial pathogens, levels equal to up to 2,500,000 X-rays are used. By-products of such radiation (radiolytic products) are potential carcinogens. Also, ionizing radiation accelerates the degradation of vitamin C and E, and may impede the formation of protein.

Top 10 Foods to buy organic

In a perfect world organic fruits and vegetables would be available and affordable all year round. In reality, for a variety of reasons, this may not be the case. However, the one billion pounds of pesticides and herbicides used on conventionally grown crops can have a serious effect on our immune and endocrine (hormonal) systems. The following is a list of foods that are often treated with the most chemicals and should therefore be a priority to buy organic. Generally the chemicals applied are known endocrine disruptors, carcinogens (cancer-causing) and neurotoxins (they cause damage to the nervous system and brain.)

1. Animal based foods	6. Pears
2. Apples	7. Spinach
3. Bell Peppers	8. Strawberries
4. Cucumbers	9. Tomatoes
5. Green Beans	10. Peaches

** For more information go to **www.stayingalivecookbook.com/links**. See list of common chemicals used on produce on page 175.

Farmers' markets

If certified organic foods aren't available in your area, the next best option is to shop for seasonal produce at a local farmers' markets or buy directly from local growers. This produce has usually been picked fresh from the field that week and is at its prime in terms of nutrient content. The variety, quality and freshness will soon have you coming back for more. These farmers are your neighbours in the local community, and are less likely to be using chemicals on a large scale. Meeting the growers is also a great opportunity to reconnect and re-form relationships based on the judgment and integrity that is often lacking in large scale productions. Local produce, because it is so seasonal, is also incredibly affordable.

Transitional

You may see the term transitional used in the organic section at the supermarket or at farmers' market. Due to the stringent regulations and procedures required for a farm to have the "certified organic" label it takes up to seven years for a farm to make it to this level. The term "transitional" is to indicate that a farm is heading towards the full "certified organic" status and portrays the good intent and principles of the farm owners, and so "transitional" is well worth supporting.

ABCs of GMOs

Did you know that up to 80 per cent of the foods on the supermarket shelf contain genetically modified organisms (GMOs)? The most common genetically engineered ingredients are canola, corn, soy, potatoes, flax and tomatoes. When you think of corn in all its forms as corn syrup, corn oil, cornmeal and cornstarch, you begin to realize how pervasive genetically modified corn is in our processed food products, from breakfast cereals, to baked goods, candy, syrups and crackers.

What are genetically modified organisms (GMOs)?

Genetically modified organisms are life-forms that have been modified, by scientists in the field of biotechnology, to enhance that organism to produce a desired result. For thousands of years farmers have used cross breeding techniques to improve food crops. By mixing the pollen of tasty potato species with that of a hardy potato variety, new varieties were produced that were both tasty and hardy. In the last 20 years however, science has been using genetic engineering techniques to achieve similar results. Usually the desired DNA (information from the gene, sometimes referred to as the blueprint of life) is injected at the cellular level and the receiving cell's natural DNA is bombarded, causing it to be permanently changed. The result is a genetically modified organism (GMO). However, this procedure is not exact-imagine shooting a shot gun and the shot spraying everywhere, with only a couple of pieces hitting the target. It may take years of repeating the process to get the desired result and it is uncertain what other genetic changes may have taken place in the process. The dramatic difference between the ancient plant breeding methods and genetic engineering (GE) is that cross pollination only worked within the same species, (ie potato plants). With genetic engineering, the DNA of any species can be injected into that of another. Fish genes can be injected into tomato cells in an effort to make the tomatoes more resistant to the cold and bacterial toxins can be injected into potato genes.

It has been scientifically understood that there is "mobile DNA" that occur naturally and transverse and exist within different species. It is thought that this is involved with natural evolution, through the mutation process. As scientists forge ahead and speed up this process, through genetic manipulation, the results for evolution are unknown. Dr G. Wald, Professor Emeritus in Biology at Harvard University and Nobel Laureate in Medicine, once stated "It is all too big and is happening too fast. So this, the central problem, remains almost unconsidered. It presents probably the largest ethical problem that science has ever had to face. Our morality up to now has been to go ahead without restriction to learn all that we can about nature. Restructuring nature was not part of the bargain. For going ahead in this direction may be not only unwise, but dangerous. Potentially, it could breed new animal and plant diseases, new sources of cancer, novel epidemics."

Why would we inject toxins into a potato?

The Colorado beetle is a voracious consumer of potato crops. The naturally occurring bacillus thuringiensis, or B.t. toxin has been used as an effective pesticide for years. When the beetle is exposed to it, it dies. Now biotechnology has made the toxin a genetic part of the potato, whenever the beetle takes a little munch it dies. But what happens to us? How are we affected when we munch on our fries and potato chips? For both the corn and potatoes containing B.t. toxin, scientists are concerned that these foods may cause allergies in certain people or poisonous effects in those using ulcer medications or antacids that reduce stomach acidity.

Why am I hearing so much about genetic engineering (GE)?

Now that you know you have been eating genetically engineered foods unwittingly, how do you feel? Many consumers are demanding to know whether their foods contain genetically modified ingredients. They feel that they are being used as human guinea pigs. Do we know what happens when we consume scientifically altered DNA on a daily basis from our food sources? The fact is that there has been no long term testing. Consumers are the long-term experiment.

How can I tell if GE ingredients are in my food?

The truth of the matter is that you can't. There is no government regulation that commands food manufacturers to disclose the use of GMOs despite the fact that a 1994 Industry Canada survey found that 83 to 94 per cent of Canadians want such products labelled. As consumers we have a right to know and concerned community and national groups have been calling for mandatory labeling.

In 1998, more than 1,300 UK schools in five council areas removed genetically engineered foods from their menus. The move, which originated at Kent County Council, stemmed from the concerns of caterers that food for schools should meet "the highest standards of safety."

Why are Britains so concerned about food safety? "Recombinant DNA technology (genetic engineering) is an inherently risky method for producing new foods," says Dr. R. Lacey, Professor of Medical Microbiology at the University of Leeds, and the food safety expert who predicted the disaster later to be called Mad Cow Disease.

What do I do now?

Fortunately, whole foods that are Certified Organic are considered safe and free from genetic engineering. Whole foods are foods without a label; vegetables, fruits, beans, grain, nuts and seeds. Organic processed foods are the next best step. The organics standards ensure that 95 per cent of ingredients must be certified organic for the food product to be labelled "organic." However, the remaining five per cent could contain GMO ingredients. Every time you shop you vote with your dollar. Now is the time to exercise your right as a consumer to vote for what's important to you. Buying organic sends a powerful message that you no longer want to unwittingly consume GE foods.

Barbequed Meats and Other Hazards

The scientific community has known for several years about two chemical reactions that take place on the barbecue that increase carcinogenic agents. The first phenomenon features Heterocyclic Amines (HCAs). Heterocyclic amines are cancer-causing agents formed from the cooking of muscle meats such as beef, pork, chicken, and fish. HCAs form when amino acids (the building blocks of protein) and creatine (a chemical found in muscles) react at high cooking temperatures. Researchers have identified 17 different HCAs resulting from the cooking of meats and fish that may pose human cancer risk.

HCAs cannot be scraped off and once eaten they become activated to attack the DNA (our set of instructions for life) of the cell, which is a possible first step in cancer development. High cooking temperatures is one of the biggest factors contributing to high levels of HCAs in meats. Frying, broiling, and barbecuing produce the largest amounts of HCAs because the meats are cooked at very high temperatures. Researchers at the National Cancer Institute (US) found that those who ate their beef medium-well or well-done had more than three times the risk of stomach cancer than those who ate their beef rare or medium-rare. Additional studies have shown that an increased risk of developing colorectal, pancreatic, and breast cancer is associated with high intakes of well-done, fried, or barbecued meats.

We all know that meats need to be cooked thoroughly and at high temperatures to reduce the risk of food poisoning. However, while oven roasting and baking lowers the levels of HCAs because of lower cooking temperatures, it doesn't solve the dilemma of how to enjoy a barbecue's delights.

The second phenomenon is a nasty "polycyclic aromatic hydrocarbon" by the name of Benzopyrene. It belongs to a family of compounds that are potential mutagens (mutation producing agents) and carcinogens! They are present in tobacco smoke, and account for parts of tobacco-related cancers in humans. We also get exposed to this agent from incomplete burning of oil, fat and organic material from cooking, industrial and car exhaust and home heating. Barbecuing our meats simply increases our exposure. When fat from the meat drips on the charcoal or heating elements, the benzopyrenes are formed. They then vapourize, adhere to soot and deposit on the surfaces of the meat. Foil can be used to counteract this effect, but that still doesn't give me the distinctive grilled flavour of a barbeque.

Fortunately, HCAs are only found in cooked muscle meats; other sources of protein , such as tofu, have very little or no HCA content naturally or when cooked. Simply learning how to marinate and grill tofu and assorted vegetables results in fantastic flavour. The key to success is in the marinade (don't even think barbequing without marinating first). Garlic, lime, tamari soy sauce and sesame oil are the features of most marinade bases I've tried. (See recipe on page 136).

Be warned, make three times the amount you have planned. Initially everyone is going to want to try it, and then they'll have to try it again to convince themselves that grilled tofu can taste this good. Hopefully after these taste-testings, there will be some left for you to enjoy.

Fish

When eating fish, there are some potential hazards you need to be aware of. Due to marine pollution over the last 50 years our oceans have become exposed to persistent chemicals and heavy metals. These pollutants accumulate in the fatty tissues of marine animals as they move up the food chain (a process called bio-accumulation). This results in some fish being more toxic than the water that surrounds them.

In an effort to reduce exposure to toxicity, I personally do not recommend fish. For those consuming it, it is a matter of finding a balance between moderate consumption (an average of two servings per week) and always focusing on quality sources.

The Environmental Protection Agency has released several warnings particularly with regard to methyl-mercury which has been shown to contribute to neurological defects in developing fetuses. Pregnant women are advised to have only ¼ cup serving of tuna per week. This powerful substance may also be affecting the neurological or immune systems of adult fish eaters.

On the other hand, it is widely known that deep sea fish (salmon, mackerel, herring, sardines) are a good source of omega-3 fatty acids, the 'healthy' essential fatty acids, which help to support our immune system. They are also a source of EPA and DHA, which are precursors to beneficial prostaglandins. In fact, the fish have produced EPA and DHA from consuming seaweeds and algae that are a natural source of omega-3 fats.

When humans consume omega 3 fatty acids, the fatty acids are also transformed into EPA and DHA. However if a body is stressed or compromised this transformation is not guaranteed. Fortunately, EPA and DHA can also be found in micro-algae supplements. These supplements are also fed to chickens to produce "omega-3" eggs. Why don't we just eat the original foods and get benefits directly?

Omega-3 fatty acids can also be obtained from organic flax seeds, hemp seeds, fresh raw walnuts, beans and green leafy vegetables. These are my preferred sources for these essential and immune-boosting fats.

Chapter Twelve:

Miracles at the Market — Cancer-Conquering Foods

Miracles at the Market – Cancer-Conquering Foods

Science is beginning to show us what ancient societies have known across the ages. Plant foods are healing foods and can even act as powerful medicines. These properties are due to "phytochemicals," phyto being Latin for plant. These plant chemicals are vast in number and have often long and complicated names. You may have heard of lycopene, resveratrol, inositol hexaphosphate (IP 6) and beta carotene. While they are not easy to pronounce, they are easy to incorporate into your daily diet. As you'll see from the recipes, these foods are featured as the ingredients of our cancer conqueror's meals.

Top 20 Power Foods

Apples
Scientists at Cornell University performed tests on human colon cancer cells and found that apple skin inhibited the growth of cancer cells by 43 per cent. Tests on liver cells were even more effective. An apple a day may indeed keep the doctor away.

Asian Mushrooms
The shiitake, reishi and maitake mushrooms have long been used in Asia to boost the immune system. Research has shown that the immune-boosting effects in the mushroom are due to complex carbohydrates called beta-glucans. Consume these mushrooms in soup, stews and gravies. They have four times the flavour of white button mushrooms and also provide protein (18 per cent of mass). The white button mushroom has no therapeutic effects and some claim that this species has cancer-causing potential (hydrazines) unless cooked. Asian mushrooms are now available in fresh and dried forms in most supermarkets.

Beans (legumes)
Botanically speaking, beans are seeds that grow in pods, and there are more than 14,000 varieties known. Even the colour of the skin on a bean is a source of antioxidants. Beans, while being an excellent source of protein, also contain protective fibre, which helps eliminate toxins. Readily available varieties include, red kidney beans, black beans, lentils, chick peas (or garbanzo beans), split peas, pinto beans and soy beans.

Blueberries
Blueberries have come out top on the list of the most powerful antioxidant foods. Not only do they pack a punch of vitamin C, which is helpful for immune system function and body repair, but they also contain the blue pigment anthocyanin, a powerful phytochemical. Other blue foods to consume include purple grapes and plums. Also the berries, plums and dark grapes contain resveratrol, which acts as an anti-oxidant and may also regulate estrogen levels. If you have been diagnosed with cancer, alcohol will not benefit your body, so consume the red-blue fruits in their whole form, as juice in moderate amounts, or de-alcoholized red wine occasionally.

Brown Rice
Grains in their whole form (not necessarily as a flour) contain both soluble and insoluble fibre, which facilitates hormone excretion and decreases the burden of

environmental toxins in the body. Grains such as oats, rye, barley, buckwheat and millet have marked inhibitory effects in the presence of carcinogens due to lignans. Studies show that lignans have both anti-tumour and anti-viral effects. It's time to move beyond wheat and discover the benefits of the other members of the grain family.

Brown rice, a staple of the macrobiotic diet, led researchers to discover the power of IP6, a component of fibre that is found in grains and legumes. Animal studies have highlighted the tumour reducing potential of IP6 in both whole food and supplement form.

Carrots

Scientists have found that cooking and puréeing carrots increases the availability of their antioxidants more than three times. Keeping the outer skin on carrots (as with other fruits and vegetables) retains numerous extra cancer-fighting compounds. Carrots belong to the "umbelliferous" group of foods, which contain rich sources of plant chemicals including beta-carotene and canthaxanthin. Other foods in this group include parsley, celery, dill, celeriac, parsnips, cumin, fennel, chervil, caraway and coriander.

Cruciferous Vegetables

The cruciferous vegetable family have long been held to have cancer prevention properties. Until recently, scientists didn't quite know why, but recent studies have shown that these vegetables help with the body's toxic waste-disposal system. Plant chemicals, such as sulforophane and indole-3-carbinol, trigger the release of a protein that causes the release of a dozen or more toxin-fighting enzymes. These enzymes either neutralize cancer-causing chemicals or help the body excrete them. Cruciferous foods include broccoli, kale, cauliflower, cabbage, brussels sprouts and watercress.

Flax Seeds

In a recent Canadian study, flax seed consumed daily was found to slow tumour growth in breast cancer patients. A muffin with 50 grams of ground flax seed was fed to participants. Those who had a flax muffin experienced statistically significant reduction in tumor growth. 50 grams of flax seed equals about two tablespoons. Flax consists of protein, oils high in beneficial omega-3 fatty acids and fibre. The lignans in the fibre are considered to be active disease fighters (see Brown Rice). Whole flax seeds can be ground using a coffee grinder (or purchased ground) and sprinkled liberally on breakfast cereals, salads or smoothies.

Garlic

It turns out that the "stinking" part of the "stinking rose" (as garlic has been traditionally called) contains the powerful immune supporting and cancer-fighting properties of garlic. When used in cooking, more than 70 sulphur-bearing compounds are released. These compounds hinder cancer cell growth and have anti-viral, anti-bacterial and anti-fungal properties.

Garlic also contains selenium, which contributes to antioxidant activity and has been shown to enhance detoxification and reduce the risk of cancer recurrence after surgery. Both the sulphur compounds and selenium are also found in the "allium" family of onions, leeks, chives, shallots and scallions. Eat them cooked in soups, stews and vegetable dishes or raw in dips, salads and salad dressings.

Ginger
This herb not only helps fight cancer, but ginger is also an anti-nausea remedy, shown to have the equivalent effect as over-the-counter drugs. It can be used to combat the nausea associated with chemotherapy. Ginger, due to some very powerful antioxidant compounds, is more potent than vitamin E, which is touted as the most powerful antioxidant.

Ginger is used extensively in Asian diets where cancer incidence is much lower and is beneficial in both fresh and powdered forms. Use in stir-fries, baking, and in boiling water as tea.

Green Tea
With more than 3,000 varieties of tea, deciding which to drink can be confusing. The good news is, studies have shown that compounds in all three types of teas (green, black, and oolong) have cancer-fighting properties. Green tea in particular contains powerful catechins and polyphenols that are being studied as tumour-reducing factors. Green tea has been shown to block mutagens (factors that damage DNA), be an antioxidant, anti-bacterial and anti-viral, and can protect against chemicals and radiation.

Buy good quality loose leaf varieties. Tea bags are made from the small, lesser quality leaves. Tea has naturally occurring caffeine and some studies indicate that this may increase its cancer-fighting effectiveness. Unless you are particularly sensitive to caffeine, two to three cups of green tea will provide you with optimum cancer-fighting potential. The Japanese and Chinese have been drinking the tea in this natural form for millennia, and definitely have the lower cancer incidences to show for it. If you are drinking more than three cups per day, consider switching to decaffeinated green tea (ensure that it's decaffeinated by a water process method) for the latter part of the day.

Seaweed
Another staple of the Asian Pacific diet, seaweeds, or sea vegetables, are extremely high in minerals, which contribute to optimum immune system function and help minimize the uptake of some toxic agents.

Edible species of seaweeds contain anti-tumour and antioxidant activities. This may be due to the presence of alginates that also protect against radiation. Try seaweeds such as kelp, kombu, dulse, nori sheets and arame. See the "How to Buy Quality Foods" section on page 71, to learn how to include them in your daily or weekly program.

Soy

Hundreds of scientific studies, are proving soybeans have anti-cancer and, anti-viral properties and that they contain protoease inhibitors that can act as antioxidants. Of the legume family, soy beans contain the highest levels of saponins, which are toxic to tumour cells and decrease tumour cell growth. Soy has come under the spotlight because it was identified as a staple in Asian diets, and some Asian communities have 80 per cent less breast and prostate cancer and less than half the ovarian and colon cancer of North Americans.

Consequently, Western researchers have taken a great interest in soy foods. Soy was found to have certain phytoestrogens and plant chemicals called isoflavones; two of these being genistein and diadzein.

In typical western fashion, science identified these "active ingredients," isolated them and has learned how to process and manufacture them. These are now sold as supplements that harness the "power" of soy foods without us having to eat the beans! Unfortunately, we don't truly know the effect of these isolated phytochemicals on the human body, taken in quantities thousands of times stronger than those normally found in food.

We do know that the Asians have been eating edamame (steamed fresh soy beans), tofu, soy milk, miso and tempeh – the latter two being very traditional fermented soy foods. They have also combined these foods with the other foods mentioned in this book, whole grains, vegetables, seaweeds, garlic, ginger and green tea. They have not been consuming soy protein shakes, powders or protein bars that are being promoted as an easy "health" fix in the West. In fact, a couple of preliminary studies have shown that isoflavone supplements increase estrogen-receptor positive breast cancer cell growth in animals. We don't know how these results apply to humans, but doctors such as Michael Murray recommend that women who have estrogen-receptor positive breast cancer should restrict soy food consumption (to less than four servings per week) and should avoid soy supplements.

In summary, soy in its traditional food form can play an important role as a cancer preventative, and as part of a cancer management program. Use as a regular ingredient, but not to the exclusion of other whole foods. Once again, the traditional forms include edamame (steamed fresh soy beans), tofu, soy milk, miso and tempeh. Avoid high consumption of foods or supplements that are made from isolated soy proteins.

Tomatoes

Extensive research has shown that tomatoes suppress cancer-producing chemicals through the existence of vitamin C and lycopene. Lycopene, a red pigment in foods, has been featured heavily in the media for reducing prostate cancer risk. Lycopene from tomatoes is made more readily available by cooking, and it also needs a little fat to be absorbed so add some olive oil. A tomato sauce or tomatoes used as a base in soups are generally recommended. Be aware, you'll also find this colourful pigment in strawberries, watermelon and pink grapefruit, so be sure to include some of these fruits too.

Turmeric

Turmeric is the dried, powdered form of a yellow plant spice related to ginger. Studies of the Indian population, where turmeric is used along with other spices in curries, have shown a decrease in incidence of some types of cancer. Turmeric can block cancer formation, acts as an antioxidant and is also a powerful anti-inflammatory. Its bright yellow colour adds visual appeal to dishes, while imparting only a mild flavour.

The Complete Nutritional Top 40

1. Apples
2. Barley
3. Berries
4. Black beans
5. Blueberries
6. Broccoli
7. Brown rice
8. Brussels sprouts
9. Cabbage
10. Carrots
11. Cauliflower
12. Chick peas
13. Chives
14. Coriander
15. Flax seeds
16. Garlic
17. Ginger
18. Green tea
19. Hemp seeds
20. Kale
21. Leeks
22. Lentils
23. Maitake mushrooms
24. Oats
25. Onion
26. Parsley
27. Pumpkin seeds
28. Plums
29. Red grapes
30. Red kidney beans
31. Reishi mushrooms
32. Rye
33. Scallions
34. Sea weed
35. Sesame seeds
36. Shiitake mushrooms
37. Soy beans
38. Split peas
39. Tomatoes
40. Turmeric

Chapter Thirteen:

Three Steps to Building a Complete Meal

Three Steps to Building a Complete Meal

It is natural to have concerns about following a new, mainly plant-based food program. Will I be getting enough protein and calcium? Will I feel full? Will I consume too many carbohydrates? In response to these frequently asked questions I have put together the **Balanced Meal Wheel.** ™

What's wrong with current food pyramids? The government food pyramids have failed. The Canada Food Guide, was first released in 1956, and yet in the new millennium North America has epidemic levels of heart disease, cancer, obesity and adult onset diabetes. Some evidence suggests that the beef, pork, egg and dairy industries have influenced the food guide content, consequently including more of these products against the recommendations of scientists for optimum public health.

Of course the food pyramids can't simply be blamed for failure of health. The population does not incorporate the suggestions (less than 10 per cent of US citizens eat their required intake of three to five vegetable servings daily) and also the nutritional quality of foods has decreased dramatically through excessive processing and unnatural food production methods.

Basically, the food pyramid hasn't been a useful tool in helping people prepare a nourishing meal or snack. We are primarily influenced by television and magazine ads for our dinner ideas, rather than thinking through, recognizing and creating well-balanced, nutritious meals.

Well, the good news is, we don't all have to be nutritionists to optimize our daily food intake as long as we understand good food and good balance.

Balanced Meal Wheel ™

CALCIUM FOODS
Soy milk - calcium fortified
Firm tofu made with calcium
Legumes
Unhulled sesame seeds
Sesame tahini
Almonds
Seaweeds: Kelp, kombu, nori, arame, dulse, hijiki, wakame
Dark green vegetables: Beet greens, bok choy, broccoli, collards, kale, mustard greens, okra, turnip greens

IMMUNE Boosters
Garlic
Ginger
Green tea
Turmeric
Fresh herbs: Burdock, dandelion, oregano
Shiitake mushrooms
Flax seed
Seaweeds: Kelp, kombu, nori, arame, dulse, hijiki, wakame

The **Balanced Meal Wheel** helps us stay optimally nourished and is a helpful guide for preparing breakfasts, lunches, dinners and snacks. Of course, the focus is on natural, good quality, whole foods, as discussed in prior chapters.

Three Steps - Putting it all together

Step One – Include at least FOUR segments in every meal for optimum nourishment.

Step Two – Aim to build meals and snacks that include an item from EACH SEGMENT in the Balanced Meal Wheel.

Step Three – Ensure you have at least ONE serving from EVERY segment EVERY DAY. If Step Two is followed you will be getting approximately five of each per day.

For example you may be preparing a vegetable stir fry for dinner. You'll start with serving it on brown rice [whole grains], but if there are only vegetables in the stir fry it won't meet the Step One criteria of including at least four segments. To meet this, use garlic and ginger in the stir fry [from the immune foods segment] and then add tofu from the beans segment. This provides a complete meal of protein (tofu), energy giving grains, vitamins and minerals from the vegetables and cancer-fighting power from the herbs.

Another example is creating a salad. Traditionally, this might just be vegetables in the form of salad greens, carrots and tomato. To make this a complete meal, you'll need to include some other segments. How about some apple pieces, [fresh fruits] and walnuts [nuts, seeds and oils] and maybe some parsley from the calcium foods segment? The salad could also be served on a "bed" of left-over grains. These new additions to the simple salad would give protein [from the nuts], vitamins and minerals from the fruits and vegetables, essential fatty acids from the walnuts and sustained energy from the carbohydrates.

Snacks can be the same, maybe you'll have a slice of sprouted whole grain bread [whole grains]. But you could also top this with almond butter [nuts, seeds and oils] and maybe eat half an apple [fresh fruit] and drink some green tea [immune boosters].

As you can see, with this kind of approach, with every single meal you are maximizing variety, flavour, nutrition and most importantly, your cancer-fighting potential.

Chapter Fourteen:

How to Buy and Use Quality Foods

How to Buy and Use Quality Foods

Now it's time to fill your kitchen with these cancer–fighting foods. Namely, beans, grains, nuts, seeds and fresh fruits and vegetables. You'll also need some teas, spices and condiments. Here are some guidelines for stocking the cupboards.

Use in Moderation

OILS

Flax Oil – Do not heat. Follow label instructions carefully. Use in salad dressings and smoothies.

Sesame Oil – Ideal for flavouring stir fries and asian salads. Must be unrefined and cold pressed.

Olive Oil – Use this versatile oil for moderate heat cooking (for frying garlic and onions etc.), salad dressings and baking. Buy unrefined and cold pressed, extra virgin olive oil.

Walnut Oil – An optional oil that can be used for baked goods. It's moderate omega–3 content adds nutritional value. Buy unrefined and cold pressed oil.

Grapeseed Oil or Ghee – Optional fats, ideal for high temperature frying as both are stable in high heats. Buy unrefined and cold pressed grapeseed oil or ghee made from organic butter.

SALT

Sea Salt with Ground Sea Kelp –Sea salt is basically de–hydrated sea water and provides a natural source of minerals. To introduce the benefits of sea–weeds (see page 64), combine ground sea kelp with sea salt (50 percent of each) and use in ALL cooking. There will be no sea–weed taste.

Do not use this mix as table salt, as this mix, uncooked, does have a sea–weed aroma.

Avoid Completely

Hydrogenated Oils – These artificially–made fats result from liquid oils being made solid at room temperature. Unfortunately, they are unrecognizable by the human body and have been shown to increase risk of heart disease and cancer. Hydrogenated oils and fats are found in margarine, cookies, commercial baked items, salad dressings and candy. Read labels carefully. Avoid anything hydrogenated and partially hydrogenated. Also avoid margarines that are "non–hydrogenated" they are still unnatural and the long–term effects of the processing on human health is unknown.

Non–Organic Butter – Organic butter, while still a source of saturated fat and naturally occurring growth hormones, reduces exposure to toxic chemicals through bioaccumulation.

Table Salt – Many brands of table salt use sugar as a cheap filler and bleaching agents for whiteness. An unprocessed sea salt is recommended and will have a slight grey hue.

Use in Moderation	Avoid Completely

SWEETENERS

Organic Brown Rice Syrup – Natural very mild sweetener from boiled–down rice grain. Use in baking, substitute equal amounts for sugar, and add to the wet ingredients.

Stevia – A herbal preparation from the leaf of a South American Stevia plant, Stevia comes in powdered or liquid form and has no detrimental effects on blood sugar. Follow instructions on package strictly for substitutions. Has unusual after taste.

Applesauce, Cinnamon and Vanilla – Natural sweeteners that can fool the taste buds into thinking something is sweeter than it is. Use in baking, cereals and smoothies. For baking with applesauce, substitute equal amounts for sugar, and add to the wet ingredients.

Organic Molasses – A sugar processing by–product. Molasses is high in calcium, iron and other minerals. Use in baking and home made breads. If chemicals have been used on the sugar crop they can accumulate in the molasses. Organic molasses is preferred.

Honey – Readily available, but not always of high quality. Use in moderation to sweeten breakfast cereals and baking. For baking, substitute equal amounts for sugar (or less), and add to the wet ingredients.

Maple Syrup – Use sparingly as this still has a high sugar content. Use in moderation to sweeten breakfast cereals and baking. For baking, substitute equal amounts for sugar (or less), and add to the wet ingredients.

White and Brown Sugar – Highly processed and stripped of any nutrients and fibre that the original sugar cane plant contains. Sugar is bleached and processed through a charred bone meal. Brown sugar is actually processed white sugar with molasses added back to it. Sugar suppresses the immune system and feeds cancer cells. Avoid totally.

Sugar cane products – A far more natural form of sweetener, these products are made from de–hydrated cane–juice, thus keeping more nutrients intact. These sugars are recommended in moderation for those improving their health regime, however they cannot be recommended for cancer patients as the pure sugar may still suppress the immune system and potentially contribute to cancer cell growth.

Use in Moderation	**Avoid Completely**

FLOURS

Spelt Flour – Made from the whole spelt grain, its lighter appearance and weight make it a good wheat substitute (both for whole wheat and white flour). Baking results have more density that white flour but are also much lighter than baking with whole wheat flour. Substitute equally for any flour in a recipe.

Whole Wheat Flour – Made from the wheat berry and ground into a flour. Using 100 percent whole wheat in a recipe can make the outcome very heavy and dense. Whole wheat flour is high in minerals and B vitamins.

White and Unbleached White Flours – Made by stripping the wheat kernel of its outer bran (high in B vitamins and minerals) and then its germ (high in vitamin E and essential fats). The resulting inner core is a simple carbohydrate with very little nutrient value. This core is ground, resulting in white flour. Often this flour is then bleached and processed for a consistency of colour and texture. Nutrients need to be added back because this product is so devoid of nutritional value. This is known as "enriched" flour.

VINEGARS

Apple Cider Vinegar – Preferable, as good quality apple cider vinegars are living foods and very natural.

Balsamic, Red Wine and Rice Vinegars – Used in moderation these add sensational flavour to dressings and grain salads. Look for quality brands with minimal preservatives and colouring agents.

White Vinegar – Highly processed and very acidic by nature. White vinegar contains no nutritional value and very little flavour.

NUTS AND SEEDS

Nuts and Seeds – Buy fresh and raw. Taste them before you buy them. Store in the fridge or freezer. They do not need to be de-frosted to be used in recipes.
If nuts in the shells are available, these are ideal and can be stored in a cool dark place. However, if used for recipes they can take a long time to shell.

Roasted and Salted Nuts and Seeds – Roasting the nuts damages the fats and makes them detrimental for health. Rancid fats also taste bad and therefore the nuts and seeds need to be heavily salted.

Roasting nuts and seeds can be done at home using the broil option on the oven. Enjoy as snacks. Make regularly in small batches to ensure freshness.

Purchase and Storage Hints

BEANS

Beans can be bought in their dried form or canned. Canned beans often haven't been soaked thoroughly. Eden Organic Canned Beans are an excellent choice.

WHOLE GRAINS

Purchase grains that have been stored in a well ventilated dry environment. Heat and light can damage the vitamins in grains. Keep in dark containers in a cool area.

Tape bay leaves to the lid and outside of the container to prevent bugs from enjoying your grains. Or store them in the fridge.

TINNED FOODS

In the past, tinned food was not recommended because lead and aluminum from the can were found to leach into the contents. Some brands (particularly organic) now line their cans with a white lining to prevent leaching. Look for this lining on tinned beans and tomato products.

Always opt for fresh fruits and vegetables rather than tinned. Frozen produce is the next best choice if fresh is unavailable. Frozen goods have usually been picked at the height of ripeness and thus have good nutritional value. They also haven't had to travel long distances while fresh.

SALAD MIX

Organic pre-washed salad greens are readily available and are highly recommended to have on hand for a daily green leafy salad fix. They can be rinsed easily before using and no chopping is required. Mix with other lettuces such as red and green romaine for a sensational salad.

SALAD DRESSINGS

Commercially prepared salad dressings may contain preservatives and hydrogenated oils. Home-made dressings provide maximum flavour and can last from five to seven days. Some natural organic dressings are available commercially; use occasionally for variety.

VEGETABLE STOCK

Look for a simple powdered vegetable stock that consists of dehydrated vegetables such as celery and carrots. Avoid stocks with any preservatives, hydrogenated oils, MSG or "natural flavours," a common disguise for MSG.

OATMEAL

Large flake? Small flake? Scotch or steel cut? Avoid three minute and quick cooking oats as these are generally treated and cooked, then dehydrated so that you can just add hot water. The processing dramatically reduces nutrient value. Any oat that takes longer than five minutes to cook on the stovetop is a good choice. Flaked oats are simply the squishing of the oat groat through a mill, whereas steel-cut oats are the oat groat chopped into pieces.

TEA

Look for good quality loose-leaf tea. Tea bags contain small fragments of tea leaves and often the tea bag has been bleached, increasing your exposure to artificial chemicals. Use the loose leaf tea with a stainless steel tea infuser. These come in individual sizes or for tea-pots and are available from tea and kitchen stores.

FLAX SEEDS

Buy in the whole form and grind as needed (or grind one-weeks worth and keep in a tightly-sealed container in the fridge). A coffee grinder is perfect for the job. Ground flax seed can also be purchased and stored in the fridge or freezer. Light, heat and oxygen can damage the beneficial, fragile oils, which is why they need be stored in a cool dark place. Ground flax seeds (but not flax oil) can be used for baking.

Whole Foods Shopping List

WHOLE GRAINS
❏ Amaranth
❏ Barley
❏ Brown rice
❏ Buckwheat and kasha
❏ Cornmeal
❏ Cracked wheat and bulgur
❏ Millet
❏ Oats
❏ Pasta (wholegrain kamut, etc.)
❏ Popcorn
❏ Quinoa
❏ Rye
❏ Wheatberries
❏ Wholegrain flours (for baking)

VEGETABLES
(local, in season are best)
❏ Beets (including tops)
❏ Broccoli
❏ Brussels sprouts
❏ Cabbage
❏ Carrots
❏ Cauliflower
❏ Celery
❏ Collards
❏ Corn on the cob
❏ Cucumber
❏ Daikon radish
❏ Kale
❏ Leafy greens
❏ Leeks
❏ Lettuce (romaine and leafy)
❏ Onions and green onions
❏ Parsley
❏ Parsnips
❏ Peas
❏ Radishes
❏ Spinach
❏ Sprouts
❏ Squash (many kinds)
❏ String beans
❏ Sweet potatoes
❏ Swiss chard
❏ Turnips (including tops)
❏ Watercress
❏ Yams

Note: Eggplant, tomatoes, potatoes, and members of the tropical nightshade family, cause allergic reactions in some people.

BEANS
❏ Adzuki beans
❏ Black beans
❏ Black-eyed peas
❏ Chick peas (garbanzo beans)
❏ Kidney beans
❏ Lentils
❏ Lima beans
❏ Mexican red beans
❏ Mung beans
❏ Pinto beans
❏ Soy beans
❏ Split beans
❏ Tempeh (frozen)
❏ Tofu

NUTS and SEEDS
(small amounts)
❏ Almonds
❏ Cashews
❏ Filberts (hazelnuts)
❏ Flax
❏ Nut butters
❏ Pecans
❏ Pumpkin seeds
❏ Sesame seeds
❏ Sunflower seeds
❏ Tahini
❏ Walnuts

SEA VEGETABLES
(excellent source of minerals and antioxidants)
❏ Agar (for thickening)
❏ Arame
❏ Dulse
❏ Hiziki
❏ Kelp
❏ Kombu
❏ Nori
❏ Wakame

UNREFINED OILS
(avoid over-heating oils, keep refrigerated, use small amounts)
❏ Flax oil
❏ Hemp oil
❏ Olive oil (extra virgin is finest quality)
❏ Sesame oil
❏ Walnut oil (for baking)

SEASONINGS
(tiny amounts)
❏ Braggs Liquid Amino Acids
❏ Miso (fermented soy product)
❏ Nutritional yeast (powder and flakes)
❏ Sea salt
❏ Spices (basil, coriander, cumin, sage, turmeric, etc. are digestive aids and act to inhibit moulds in foods stored for several days)
❏ Soy sauce
❏ Vegetable salt
❏ Vegetable broth powder

SWEETENERS
(small amounts)
❏ Apple butter
❏ Apple sauce
❏ Barley malt (liquid or powder)
❏ Brown rice syrup
❏ Carob powder
❏ Fruit juice or purée
❏ Maple syrup/honey/molasses
❏ Organic soy yogurt

BEVERAGES
(drink warm in winter, cooler in summer)
❏ Green tea
❏ Herb teas (peppermint, chamomile, rosehip, licorice, etc.)
❏ Nut milks
❏ Oat milk
❏ Rice milk
❏ Spring or glacier water
❏ Soymilk (made from whole organic soybeans - unsweetened)

CONVENIENCE FOODS
Grain Products
❏ Cereals, wholegrain (cracked, flaked and puffed)
❏ Chapattis, wholegrain
❏ Muesli (Swiss breakfast cereal)
❏ Pita bread, whole grain rice cakes (a light snack)
❏ Tortillas, corn
❏ Wholegrain, sprouted breads and wraps

High-Protein Products
❏ Beans, canned (no sugar or chemicals)
❏ Veggie burger patties (frozen)
❏ Chili mix
❏ Falafel mix
❏ Nut butters (almond, cashew)
❏ Sesame paste (tahini)

Soups
❏ Organic soups in boxed packaging
❏ Dry mix package soups with only natural ingredients
❏ Vegetable bouillon cubes

Chapter Fifteen:

Cooking Basics

How To Cook Grains

If you've ever had a "bad brown rice experience," of chewy gluggy grains, the truth is you've probably vowed never to eat them again. For guaranteed fluffy, light and enjoyable grains, follow the instructions below every time.

Use 4 cups of water to 1 cup of grain. Bring water to the boil. Add a pinch of sea salt (or your sea salt and ground sea kelp mix) to the water. Add the grain slowly, cover pot tightly, lower heat to medium-low and simmer until cooking time is complete (see chart below). Do not remove the lid or stir the grain while it is cooking. Save left over liquid for soup stock, as it is high in nutrients.

If using the grain for a grain salad, rinse the grain in a colander or wire strainer under cold water, drain and store in the fridge.

You can cook enough grain for four days. It can be quickly reheated whenever you like.

The following times work best for cooking with a covered pot.

Grain	Cook Time (minutes)
Barley	30
Brown rice	45
Buckwheat/Kasha	20
Cracked wheat	15
Kamut	55
Millet	40
Quinoa	15
Rolled oats	10
Wheat berries	60-90
Wild rice	45

How To Cook Beans

Time is one of our scarcest resources and cooking beans from scratch isn't always an option. Always have some good quality canned beans on hand to prepare a quick meal. Home cooked beans are much cheaper and can also be done in large batches and stored in two cup servings in the freezer for easy use later.

Presoak dry beans overnight in a bowl. Pour off the soak water, as this will minimize gas problems. Put beans in a pot with at least double their volume of water. With the lid on, bring beans to a boil and then turn down to simmer. Cook until beans are so soft you can squash them with your tongue against the roof of your mouth.

Bean type	Cook Time (hours)
Adzuki beans	1½ hrs
Black beans	1½ - 2
Black-eyed peas	1 - 1½
Garbanzos (Chickpeas)	2 - 3
Kidney beans	1½ - 2
Red lentils	20 mins
Lentils green/brown	½ - 1
Lima beans (lg)	2
Lima beans (sm)	1 - 1½
Navy beans	2
Peas (split)	½
Peas (whole)	1
Pinto beans	1 - 1½
Soybeans	2½ - 3

Beans keep well in the fridge for two to three days, especially if some spices are added, and are easily reheated. They also freeze well in small containers or baggies.

To pressure-cook beans, place in cooker and cover with water (three parts water to one part beans). Add 1 tablespoon of oil to prevent foaming. Times for pressure-cooked beans will be about ¼ that of the times given above for a covered stove-top pot.

How to Cook Vegetables

Vegetables can be steamed in 10 minutes or less. Choose two or three for colour and taste appeal. Wash. Cut harder ones such as carrots into small, bite-size chunks. Place in steamer basket in large pot. Bring water in the bottom of the pot to a boil, reduce heat and simmer until done, ensuring the water doesn't dry up completely. Steamed vegetables should not be overcooked, but should be slightly crispy. Season with sea salt, soy sauce, gravy made with arrowroot or oat flour, spices, etc. Save the steaming water for soup.

GREENS – Dark leafy greens are important, especially for calcium. Watch them closely as they take less time to cook. Boil or steam them for only two to three minutes.

BAKED VEGETABLES – Most appropriate during the fall and winter, bake vegetables with or without oil. Baking winter or summer squash is easy. Just wash, cut in half, lightly oil skin and place flat side down on baking sheet. Bake in oven at 350 F (180 C) until soft.

Times: summer squash = 20 minutes, winter squash = 30-45 minutes, sweet potato or yam = one hour.

International Flavours

If you start experimenting with different sauces, dressings and grain salads the following international spices will help you achieve the desired results.

Mexican

Chili, cumin fresh or dried, salsa, cilantro, bell peppers, black and red beans, brown rice.

Italian

Fresh or dried basil, oregano, tomatoes, bell peppers, white beans, barley, bulghar wheat.

Asian

Limes, lime juice, sesame oil, sesame seeds, cashews, water chestnut, radishes, carrots, bean sprouts, soy sauce, tofu, soy beans.

African

Cumin, coriander, yams, corn, peas, lentils, garbanzo beans, peanuts, apricots, raisins.

Indian

Curry, cardamom, garam marsala, black mustard, caraway seeds, lentils, spinach, brown rice.

Thai

Lemongrass, red curry paste, green curry paste, lime juice, soy sauce, coconut milk, peanuts, bean sprouts, tofu, rice noodles or brown rice.

Chapter Sixteen:

Phase One Menu Plan

Phase One Menu Plan

If you are making a transition directly from the standard North American diet of processed foods, high saturated fat and low fibre, I advise starting at Phase One. This has many benefits:

✔ It allows your body time to adjust to the high-fibre nature of these new foods.

✔ Slow change over a longer period of time has been shown, scientifically, to lead to sustained lifestyle change – that means your future will reflect healthy choices on a daily basis.

✔ Phase One has been designed with working people in mind. It features commonly available lunches such as sandwiches and easy-to-re-heat foods.

Taking time to transition is important, since sometimes it can be just too much to change everything at once. Phase One focuses on regular breakfasts and some new lunch and snack ideas. Dinners are a lower priority in this phase. You may wish to continue making family favourites, ensuring that they are made from organic meats and produce.

Follow Phase One for four weeks, or until you are feeling comfortable with your ability to prepare and enjoy the breakfast, lunch and snack suggestions.

Phase One Focus Points

DAILY GREEN SALAD   Try large side salads, fortified with almonds, walnuts, hazelnuts, chickpeas, marinated tofu cubes and sunflower and pumpkin seeds. Pumpkin seeds are high in zinc and good for strengthening immunity. Nuts and seeds also provide essential fatty acids (EFAs). Green leafy vegetables provide healthy fats as well as chlorophyll. Try homemade dressings using flax oil (keep refrigerated).

SUGAR REDUCTION   One of the challenges of reducing sugar foods and refined flours is that we are "addicted" to the sugar high and feeling of energy that it gives us. Unfortunately, there is often a "low" that is experienced several hours after consuming sugar products. Because we want the "high" feeling again our body starts craving another sugar hit. Sugar is eliminated in this program because of this effect and also because it rapidly decreases immunity for up to five hours afterwards. Therefore continual consumption of sugar and refined foods (white flour, pastas, baked goods etc.) results in a dramatically compromised immune system.

The easiest way to make this transition is to introduce complex carbohydrates in the form of whole grains. The stomach has to work harder to digest them and the sugar is released slowly into the bloodstream, therefore energy is sustained over longer periods of time. Eating whole foods results in less sugar cravings and provides optimum nourishment for the body.

WHOLE GRAINS

Another Phase One focus is to transition from white flour foods to whole wheat or whole grain versions (such as sprouted grain breads, kamut pasta, wholewheat pasta, oatmeal etc) and to experiment with grains in their whole form such as brown rice, wild rice and barley.

These are easy to incorporate for breakfasts, lunches and some dinners.

Breakfast suggestions
Store bought cereals can be high in fats and sugars, try un-toasted varieties or whole grain cereals such as oatmeal, rice or millet. Stir in raisins, applesauce, blueberries or banana etc.

Ground flax can be added daily to cereal for essential fatty acids. Keep in fridge or freezer.

Focus on a standard daily breakfast during the week of oatmeal or a smoothie to maximize energy and nutrition, with a break on weekends to enjoy some alternatives.

Lunch suggestions
Whole grain bread, trying different flours. Oat, rice, buckwheat, millet, soy etc. Spread fresh breads with pumpkin seed butter, nut butter, or hummus. For larger lunches also include leftover bean soups or casseroles.
For lunch alternatives try whole grain pasta or wild rice salads. Use other grains too, such as barley in tabbouleh.

FRUITS AND VEGETABLES

You've heard it before and you're about to hear it again: Eat more fruits and vegetables. Phase One will be significantly more successful if you can form a habit of eating more of these wonderful fresh, whole food options. Adding more to each meal is one way of increasing your intake, and fruits and veggies make delicious, quick snacks.

Snack suggestions
✔ veggie sticks and hummus or bean dip

✔ fresh fruit with fresh, raw (or lightly home roasted) nuts and seeds

✔ raisins, dates, cranberries, prunes etc. with fresh, raw (or lightly home roasted) nuts and seeds

✔ veggie sticks and fresh salsa

✔ Try a new vegetable each week, for example, bok choy, artichokes, kale and collard greens. Check the whole foods shopping list on page 76 for more options.

DAIRY AWARENESS

Humans are the only animals that insist on consuming another animal's milk after weaning. In fact, we have refused to be weaned at all. Generally in North America we consume too many dairy products as convenient high-protein foods, often to the exclusion of more nourishing, disease-fighting foods.

Modern dairy production results in bioaccumulation of agricultural chemicals that animals are exposed to in their feed. Studies as far back as the 1960s showed that pesticide residues in dairy may be up to 35 times those found on potatoes and 14 times the pesticides found on cereals and grains.

Milk, cheese, yogurt and other dairy products can also contain the artificial growth hormones and antibiotics used daily in dairy farms. When you stop to think what milk actually is-baby food for a 90-pound calf meant to grow into a 400-pound cow in one year-it's no wonder we have weight management problems in our milk-drinking society! To serve its purpose cow's milk is naturally high in protein, fat and growth hormones (one of which is identical to a human growth hormone IGF-1). These natural factors are found in organic cow's milk too.

Not surprisingly, excessive dairy consumption has been linked to reproductive cancers such as breast, ovarian and prostate cancer and more research, indicating the affect of these additional hormones on our health, is expected to come out in future studies.

For a more complete discussion on dairy and disease by Robert Kradjian, MD, retired Chief of Surgery, Breast Cancer Division, Seton Medical Center, read The Milk Letter, A Letter To My Patients, at: **www.stayingalivecookbook.com/links**

Assess the quality and quantity of any milk, cheese or yogurt you consume. Other cultures, with lower cancer rates, generally eat small amounts of naturally fermented dairy (such as kefir or natural yogurt) or, as in Asian cultures, consume little or no dairy at all.

Worried about getting enough calcium? Don't worry, calcium is readily available in a variety of foods. Refer to the Balanced Meal Wheel (page 69) for help adding calcium-rich foods to your diet. Eliminating alcohol and coffee, reducing salt and sugar, and doing regular weight-bearing exercise also helps with calcium retention, which results in bone strength.

Good dairy alternatives are available. Try using almond, oat, soy or rice milks. Look for soy milks made from organic whole soy beans. Rotate milks for variety and flavour, avoid sugars in the ingredients, or sweeten at home with pure vanilla essence.

Experiment with soy yogurts and cheeses for convenience foods. While these are still highly processed and are not recommended for daily consumption, they are worth having on hand to convert family favourites into healthier meals.

CUT COFFEE, STIMULANTS AND HYDROGENATED OILS

Hydrogenated oils lurk in many processed foods. They are unnatural for the human body and studies link them to heart disease and cancer. Check your cupboards for foods that contain "hydrogenated" anything. Flax oil kept in the freezer can be used as a margarine/butter substitute, or use almond butter or tahini (sesame seed butter) as a base for toast etc.

Transition from coffee by having half de-caffeinated coffee and half regular for four weeks, then switch to fully de-caffeinated. From here the addiction should be broken and you can comfortably choose healthier options-try green or chai tea (Tazo and Stash tea bags are good brands for flavour) with a shot of steamed soy milk, herbal teas and specialty coffee substitutes, or even organic Swiss water de-caf coffee on occasion.

A WORD ABOUT SUPPORT

Since your diagnosis, you have probably heard this statement one hundred times from friends and family: "If there's anything I can do, let me know." If people have asked if they can be of any help, you might consider requesting they make one soup or a standard favourite recipe per week. Most people are thrilled to be able to help in this way and can drop off the food in suitable freezer containers. The truth is, most people do really want to help and asking them to prepare one item per week can be manageable on their part and they will be making a contribution to your healing.

Phase One Sample Days

	Day 1	**Day 2**	**Day 3**
Breakfast	Cure-All Oatmeal and ⅓ cup fresh or frozen blueberries Green tea Fresh fruit (optional)	Nutty Granola and ⅓ cup fresh or frozen blueberries Green tea Fresh fruit (optional)	Cure-All Oatmeal and ⅓ cup fresh or frozen blueberries Green tea Fresh fruit (optional)
Snack 1	Fruit and a handful of nuts Green tea	Muffin with almond nut butter Green tea	Fruit and handful spicy roasted beans Green tea
Lunch	Sandwich on sprouted whole grain bread with hummus and fresh bean sprouts Fresh fruit Naturally sweet herbal tea	Leftovers — Vegetarian Chili on grains Fresh fruit Naturally sweet herbal tea	Sandwich on sprouted whole grain bread with hummus Amazing Mango Salad Naturally sweet herbal tea
Snack 2	Hummus with baby carrots and vegetable sticks Green tea	Fruit and a handful of nuts Green tea	Muffin with almond nut butter Green tea
Dinner	Vegetarian Chili Sensational Spring Salad Keep leftovers for lunch	Stir Fry with Broccoli Amazing Mango Salad Chop up extra carrots, peppers and celery and put in a baggie for hummus snacks during week	Eat out order... A large green garden salad and a vegetarian entrée that appeals to you

** soups, muffins, stews and grain salads are interchangeable. This menu plan is to be used as a guide. Having variety will help you stick with the plan.

Need dessert? Sometimes we feel like a little something sweet after dinner. Be warned that having sweets soon after a meal can contribute to gas and bloating. So be sure to wait 20 minutes or so after your meal. Good, sweet choices include fresh fruit, two or three dates or repeating a snack such as a muffin or small smoothie. Ideally these should be consumed throughout the day so the energy is burned and not stored as fat.

All of these menu plan items are ideal for health. If you have a larger appetite, large servings are recommended and snacks can be repeated as required. Be sure to check in with the Balanced Meal Wheel (page 69) to make sure you are maximizing your meal value.

Chapter Seventeen:

Phase Two Menu Plan

Phase Two Menu Plan

Before you start on Phase Two, check in to see that you are, on a daily basis, covering the important focus points of Phase One.

✔ Are you having leafy greens or a green salad every day?

✔ Have you switched to whole grains and are you comfortable cooking whole grains such as brown rice and barley?

✔ Have you assessed your dairy consumption and experimented with high-protein alternatives such as bean dips?

✔ Have you noticed a reduction in sugar cravings (this can take four to eight weeks)?

✔ Have you increased your fresh fruit consumption and tried different snack ideas?

Great! Now is the time to fine tune and add some more power to the program. Phase Two incorporates more grains in their whole form, with a focus on beans, nuts and seeds and introduces some new dinner ideas. Also, gentle cleansing is recommended at this point to assist the liver and to promote your healing process. For this I recommend either a greens powder, or daily vegetable juicing. For more information see page 177.

This is also a phase of really testing what you like and what works for you. The Phase Two plan is also ideal as a cancer prevention program as it incorporates more whole foods (less breads and muffins) with nutrient-rich super foods, such as the greens powder and sea vegetables.

Follow Phase Two for four weeks if you will be moving on to Phase Three. Make Phase Two your lifestyle if disease prevention is your goal.

Phase Two Focus Points

If you've been experiencing a little gas in Phase One, you'll definitely need to focus on the next point. You'll be amazed at the difference strengthening your digestive system can have. After we reach the age of 50, stomach acid levels drop off resulting in weak digestion, low energy levels and potential malnourishment.

DIGESTIVE AIDS

Having something warm, bitter or sour before a meal stimulates production of the stomach's digestive juices. Try a little lemon juice in warm water, or some apple cider vinegar in water. The Japanese tradition of green tea before and with a meal is also an option. Peppermint and chamomile teas also aid digestion.

The worst thing for digestion is a large glass of iced water! When at restaurants order a hot water with a squeeze of lemon before your meal.
Digestive enzymes can be purchased from health food stores if the above ideas do not work well for you. If you have a history of stomach ulcers, buy an enzyme complex with little or no hydrochloric acid (HCl).

Keeping fruit separate from meals is often helpful but not always necessary. And remember Grandma's advice, chew slowly!

BEANS, NUTS AND SEEDS

Start to implement bean, tofu or split pea recipes three times a week. These are high in protein, fibre and cancer-fighting properties.

Many of the greatest bean dishes and combinations are from around the world, so think ethnic! Try Japanese miso soups, split pea soup, Middle Eastern falafels and wraps, African chickpea stews, Chinese tofu veggie stir-frys, Mexican black bean chilies and Indian lentil curries and soups. Serve any of these with a grain of your choice.

GRAINS IN THEIR WHOLE FORM

This means grains that are not milled into flour or made into breads. Grains in their whole form include brown rice, wheat berries, barley, kamut and quinoa. Whole grains have disease-fighting properties. The supplement IP-6 is derived from brown rice (a major staple of the macrobiotic diet). Due to their fibre and lignan content, grains such as oats, rye, barley buckwheat and wheat have marked inhibitory effects in the presence of carcinogens. Lignans have been shown to be anti-tumour and anti-viral.

A delicious option is manna bread. A sprouted grain bread that is dehydrated and considered a "living food." This rich dense bread has a cake-like texture and is delicious with nut butters. It can be purchased from health and whole foods markets.

Dinner suggestions

Remember, keep in mind to rotate or incorporate new grains for a broader range of minerals and fibre. Try recipes with millet, buckwheat, quinoa and barley. Serve soups, salads and stews on a "bed of grains" – a chef's term for using up leftover grains found in the fridge!

SEA KELP OR SEA GREENS

Incorporate seaweeds as much as possible. Add a small amount (one teaspoon) to soups, stews, casseroles or when cooking beans. This is a simple addition to any recipes you already have. Seaweeds have healing properties and supply valuable minerals such as calcium. Common seaweeds are kelp, dulse, kombu, nori and arame.

As mentioned earlier, mix 50 per cent iodized sea salt and 50 per cent ground sea kelp and use in all cooking. Kelp is very high in calcium, has iodine for thyroid function and is high in minerals required for good immune function. Don't forget that most regular table salt contains sugar.

GENTLE DETOXIFICATION

Liver Cleanse - I recommend a gentle liver cleanse to help reduce the load of toxicity from the environment on the liver, and to jumpstart the healing process. Be aware that symptoms such as headaches and skin outbreaks may occur as your body detoxifies. These symptoms should be minimal if the Phase One whole foods diet has been followed.

Cleansing suggestions

a. a daily greens drink (TrueGreens) (see Sally's Superfood Smoothie recipe on page 163 and order details on page 177), OR

b. use of Swedish bitters (Gallexier brand Artichoke Formula has a non-alcohol base) as suggested on the label, at each meal, OR

c. a cleansing vegetable juice, however watch for hypoglycemic tendencies.

Phase Two Sample Days

	Day 1	**Day 2**	**Day 3**
Breakfast	Stainmaster Breakfast Green tea Fresh fruit (optional)	Cure-All Oatmeal and ⅓ cup fresh or frozen blueberries Green tea Fresh fruit (optional)	Stainmaster Breakfast Green tea Fresh fruit (optional)
Snack 1	Brad's Daily Supersmoothie	Sally's Superfood Smoothie	Fruit and a handful of nuts Green tea
Lunch	Squeeze of lemon juice in ½ cup warm water Mildly Spiced Split Pea Soup on Grains Fresh fruit Green tea	Squeeze of lemon juice in ½ cup warm water Pure Medicine Salad with Mildly Spiced Split Pea Soup Fresh fruit Green tea	Squeeze of lemon juice in ½ cup warm water Speedy Tomato Basil Soup Avocado Salad with Warm Vinaigrette Green tea
Snack 2	Black Bean Dip with baby carrots and vegetable sticks	Fruit and a handful of nuts Green tea	Brad's Daily Supersmoothie
Dinner	Green tea Squeeze of lemon juice in ½ cup warm water Indonesian Grain Salad *Pure Medicine Salad	Squeeze of lemon juice in ½ cup warm water Spicy Peanut Tempeh with Satay Sauce Indonesian Grain Salad	Squeeze of lemon juice in ½ cup warm water Mel's Tex Mex Tamale Pie Spring Salad Sensation Salad

*Remember to keep leftovers for lunches the next day and make large salads to last two to three days. Keep dressings separate so that salads last longer. Cover and seal salads tightly.

Chapter Eighteen:

Phase Three Menu Plan

Phase Three Menu Plan

Before you start on Phase Three check in to see that, on a daily basis, you are covering the important focus points of Phases One and Two.

✔ Are you eating leafy greens every day?

✔ Have you switched to whole grains and are you comfortable cooking whole grains such as brown rice, millet and barley?

✔ Have you assessed your dairy consumption and experimented with high protein alternatives such as bean dips?

✔ Have you noticed a reduction in sugar cravings (this can take four to eight weeks)

✔ Have you increased your fresh fruit consumption and tried different snack ideas?

✔ Is your digestion improving? (less gas and bloating)

✔ Have you bought and used some seaweed and added ground kelp to your cooking salt?

✔ Have you tried new recipes using beans, tofu, nuts and seeds?

✔ Are you doing some gentle internal cleansing (greens powder, Swedish bitters or vegetable juicing)?

Congratulations, you've come a long way and your body is being given the optimum nutrients for healing. These final recommendations come from observing some of the healthiest people I know. They have made health and longevity their main focus. Consider implementing some or all of these factors at your own pace.

Phase Three Focus Points
JUICING

Juicing is a powerful way of extracting phytonutrients, vitamins, minerals and enzymes in any easily digestible and consumable form. Because the fibres are usually removed with most juicers, avoid juicing too many fruits, as you will end up with predominantly simple fruit sugars, which can affect blood sugar levels and can slowly deplete pancreatic function. In general, juicing all kinds of vegetables is favourable, especially adding green ingredients such as parsley or kale. Sweetening with a piece of fruit is OK as long as it is just one out of a long list of vegetable ingredients. Drink eight to 16 ounces of vegetable juice daily. I must warn you that making up your own vegetable juice recipes can result in simply undrinkable disasters. Check Recommended Resources on page 177 for good juicing recipe books.

RAW AND LIVING FOODS

Generally we eat too many cooked foods in our society. Cooked foods have their benefits. They are easily digested and have a warming effect. However, raw foods retain their enzymes, which can assist with digestion and provide a "living" element to our nutrition. I highly recommend implementing more raw foods (you've been doing it already with a daily green salad and fresh fruits) and experimenting with some home-sprouted grains and beans.

Use your body as a guide, sometimes during a cold winter it is natural to desire more cooked food, while in the spring we are inclined to eat more salads and lighter fare.

Miso and sauerkraut are "live" fermented foods that are created by bacterial activity (in a similar fashion to yogurt). These can be used as condiments. Some people like to spread miso on toast to have with soups, make miso gravy and salad dressings, or use it to flavour soups. Because it is "live," add it to a soup once the pot has been removed from the heat, so that the valuable enzymes are retained and not damaged by the heat.

Try good quality sauerkraut from health food stores. Also experiment with beet and carrot varieties for extra beta-carotene. Cabbage helps cleanse the liver of carcinogens. Only one to two tablespoons per day is required (or every other day). For more books on raw and living foods see Recommended Resources on page 177.

Phase Three Sample Days

	Day 1	**Day 2**	**Day 3**
Breakfast	Stainmaster Breakfast Green tea Fresh fruit (optional)	Cure-All Oatmeal and ⅓ cup fresh or frozen blueberries Green tea Fresh fruit (optional)	Stainmaster Breakfast Green tea Fresh fruit (optional)
Snack 1	Super VJ	Fruit and handful of nuts Green tea	Super VJ
Lunch	Squeeze of lemon juice in ½ cup warm water Medicinal Miso Soup Sensational Spring Mix Salad Fresh fruit Green tea	Squeeze of lemon juice in ½ cup warm water Medicinal Miso Soup Beet and Barley Salad Fresh fruit Green tea	Squeeze of lemon juice in ½ cup warm water Brown Rice and Black Bean Hash wrapped in whole wheat tortilla with salsa Fresh fruit Green tea
Snack 2	Sally's Superfood Smoothie	Super VJ	Brad's Daily Supersmoothie
Dinner	Squeeze of lemon juice in ½ cup warm water Beet and Barley Salad Four Greens and Walnut Sauté Peach and Raspberry Cobbler	Squeeze of lemon juice in ½ cup warm water Brown Rice and Black Bean Hash Spring Salad Sensation Peach and Raspberry Cobbler	Squeeze of lemon juice in ½ cup warm water Italian Fasta Pasta Salad Ratatouille Pizza

Scrumptious Soups

Two-to-Ten Split Pea Soup

Marie: I love soups and as I live alone I usually make a batch and freeze portions to make for easy meals at the end of the work day. This one, I call my "Two-to-Ten" soup. It is just good old fashioned green pea soup (without the old fashioned ham hock!).

    2 cups (500 ml) of split green peas
    10 cups (2.5 L) of water
    3 large carrots
    3 large onions
    3 Tbsp (45 ml) olive oil
    1 bay leaf
    1 tsp (5 ml) Summer savory

Chop the carrots and onions and sauté them in the olive oil for 3 or 4 minutes. Add the split peas, water and seasoning and bring to a boil. Reduce heat to allow the soup to simmer, stirring frequently for about 1 hour or until the peas have "melted." Season to taste and enjoy. Great the next day!

Serves 8

Vegetable Lentil Soup

Marie: This is another easy favourite that freezes well. It calls for Rutabaga, but I call them Swedes. Look for them in the Fall with the root vegetables.

    3 Tbsp (45 ml) olive oil
    2 large onions
    3 cups (750 ml) carrots, chopped
    1 cup (250 ml) red lentils, rinsed in cold water
    2 cups (500 ml) rutabaga
    ½ tsp (2 ml) thyme
    ½ tsp (2 ml) Summer savory
    1 bay leaf
    4 cups (1 L) organic vegetable broth
    1 14 oz can (454 ml) chopped tomatoes with juice

Sauté carrots, onion and rutabaga in olive oil for a few minutes. Add the lentils, seasoning and vegetable broth and bring to a boil. Reduce heat and add the tomatoes and simmer for about 1 hour or until vegetables are tender. Season to taste.

Serves 6

Mild Curried Ginger and Carrot Soup

Mel: I enjoy the slight zestiness the curry gives this soup. In addition, the soup provided necessary calcium. As always the ginger was helpful for my nausea.

2 tsp (10 ml) olive oil
2 cloves garlic, finely chopped
1 medium yellow onion, chopped
2 Tbsp (30 ml) ginger root, grated or minced
1 tsp (5 ml) ground coriander
½ tsp (2 ml) ground cumin
¼ tsp (1 ml) curry powder
½ tsp (1 ml) salt
½ tsp (1 ml) pepper
4 cups (1 L) carrots, chopped
3 cups (750 ml) vegetable stock
2 cups (500 ml) low fat milk or enriched soy milk
½ cup (60 ml) chopped fresh cilantro

In a large saucepan, heat the oil and over medium heat cook the garlic, onion, ginger root, coriander, cumin and curry powder, salt and pepper. This releases the aroma of the curry. Cook until onions are soft, five to ten minutes. Stir in the carrots until well coated, add the stock and bring to a boil. Reduce heat, cover and cook until carrots are very soft, 20 to 30 minutes.

Turn the heat off. Using a hand blender, carefully blend the soup until creamy. (If no hand blender is available, transfer the soup in batches to a blender. This gives best results if you're having company over.)

Return the pot to the heat and add milk or soymilk, reheat gently until just hot. Serve in bowls and decorate with cilantro.

Serves 4

Balanced Meal Wheel ™

CALCIUM FOODS
Soy milk - calcium fortified
Firm tofu made with calcium
Legumes
Unhulled sesame seeds
Sesame tahini
Almonds
Seaweeds: Kelp, kombu, nori, arame, dulse, hijiki, wakame
Dark green vegetables: Beet greens, bok choy, broccoli, collards, kale, mustard greens, okra, turnip greens

IMMUNE Boosters
Garlic
Ginger
Green tea
Turmeric
Fresh herbs: Burdock, dandelion, oregano
Shiitake mushrooms
Flax seed
Seaweeds: Kelp, kombu, nori, arame, dulse, hijiki, wakame

Spring Salad Mix Sensation page 110

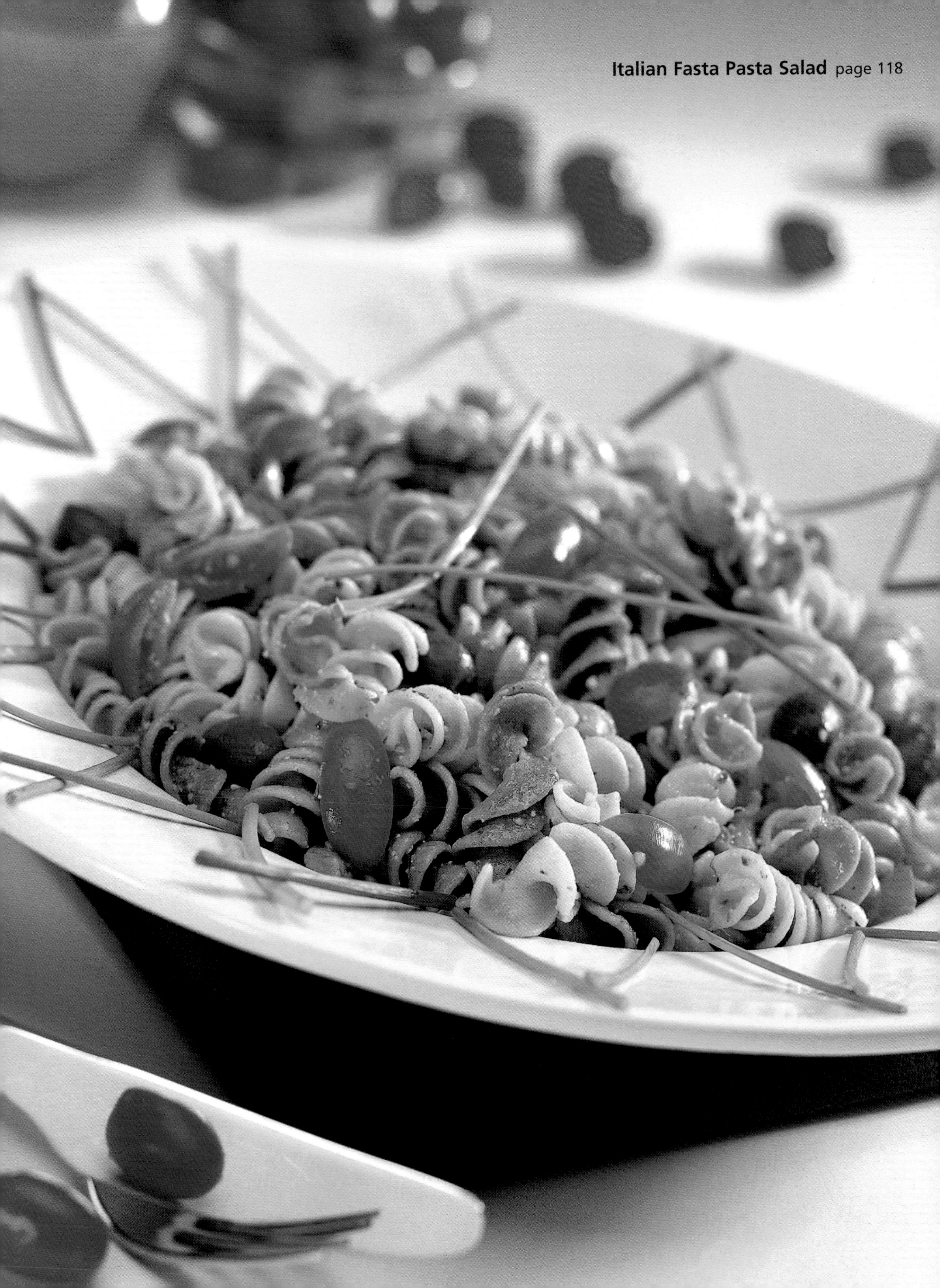

Italian Fasta Pasta Salad page 118

Creamy Roasted Garlic Tomato Soup page 102

Potato Corn Chowder

Mel: An old standby, I have loved this soup for years. It is a nice comfort food. It is also very easy to make because the ingredients are always around the house.

2 cups (500 ml) corn niblets
2 tsp (10 ml) olive oil
1 cup (250 ml) onion, chopped
½ cup red bell pepper, finely chopped
1 tsp (5 ml) garlic, finely chopped
1 cup (250 ml) potato, peeled and diced
1 ½ cups (375 ml) vegetable stock
2 Tbsp (30 ml) whole wheat flour
1 ½ cups milk or soy milk
¼ tsp (1 ml) tamari soy sauce
Salt and pepper to taste

Place 1 cup of the corn in a blender, puree and then add back to the unblended corn.

In a large saucepan, heat the oil and sauté the onion, garlic and red pepper until soft, around 5 minutes. Add the stock and diced potato. Bring to the boil and then lower heat and simmer for 15 minutes. Add the corn, cook for 5 minutes. Using a whisk, stir in the flour until ingredients are evenly coated. Slowly add milk, while stirring continuously, add tamari soy sauce and pepper. Heat until just thickened and serve.

Serves 4

Black-Eyed Bean Soup

Dennis: This is a meal all by itself and is wonderful and nourishing on a cold winter day, for lunch or dinner.

1 cup (250 ml) dried black-eyed beans
1 Tbsp (15 ml) olive oil
2 medium onions, chopped
2 medium carrots, chopped
1 small sweet potato
1 medium turnip, chopped
2 sticks celery, chopped
1 medium zucchini, chopped
2-14oz cans (796 ml) crushed tomatoes
2 cups (500 ml) of water
1 large vegetable stock cube, crushed
2 Tbsp (30 ml) tomato paste

Cover beans with cold water in a large bowl; stand, covered, overnight. Drain beans. Heat oil in pan, add onions, carrots, sweet potato, turnip and celery, continually stir for five minutes. Add beans, zucchini, crushed tomatoes. Add stock cube, water and the tomato paste. Simmer covered for approx: 1½ hours or until beans are tender.

Serves 6

Mildly Spiced Split Pea Soup

Dennis: This soup is a hearty meal all by itself, and everyone I've served it to loves it. It's a new twist on an old favourite.

4 cups (1 L) water
1½ cups (375 ml) dry split peas
2 large onions chopped
4 scallions chopped
4 garlic cloves, finely chopped
6 sprigs of cilantro, chopped
1 green pepper, chopped
1 tsp (5 ml) ground cumin
½ tsp (2 ml) curry powder
½ tsp (2 ml) powdered ginger
2 Tbsp (30 ml) olive oil
2 large stalks celery, chopped
½ tsp (2 ml) unrefined sea salt
1 tsp (5 ml) pepper

In a large saucepan, bring water to a boil. Add split peas, and reduce heat to low. Cook for 50 minutes or until they begin to disintegrate. Add more water, for a thinner consistency, if desired. Add the remaining ingredients, except salt and pepper. Cook over low heat for 30 minutes. Season with salt and pepper.

Serves 4

Mild Indian Dahl

Surround your big bowl of dahl and rice with little plates of sweet and savoury items such as banana with lightly-roasted coconut, green apple slices with raisins, or steamed broccoli and cauliflower for added nutrients. The raw items help provide enzymes for digestion. Dahl is best served with brown rice.

1 cup (250 ml) red or brown lentils or moong dahl
4 cups (1 L) water
2 Tbsp (30 ml) olive oil
2 onions, chopped
2 cloves garlic
2 tsp (10 ml) cumin seeds
1 tsp (5ml) ground turmeric
2 tsp (10 ml) grated root ginger
1 tsp (5 ml) garam masala
1 tsp (5 ml) salt
2-3 tomatoes, finely chopped

Boil the lentils in the water until tender and mushy - about 30 minutes for red lentils.

In another pan, heat the oil and the cumin seeds, ginger and tumeric over moderate heat and after 1 minute add the onion and garlic and cook until the onion is tender. At least 10 minutes.

Stir in the garam masala and the salt and remove from the heat.
Add the tomatoes plus the onion mixture to the lentils when they are soft, and simmer together for 5 minutes. Boil fast if mixture needs thickening, or add more water if it is too thick. (Aiming for spaghetti sauce-like consistency).
Taste and adjust seasonings. Serve immediately with rice and side dishes.

Serves 8-10

Borscht

Borscht is an incredibly powerful soup. Its rich colour signifies the presence of powerful carotenes (plant pigments) that have been shown to prevent the body from aging, environmental damage and disease. Use your food processor to reduce chopping time from 20 minutes by hand, to just 5 -8 minutes.

1-2 small beets
1 small onion
1 medium potato
1 carrot
1 celery stalk
1 cup (250 ml) shredded red cabbage
2 cups (500 ml) vegetable stock
1 cup (250 ml) crushed tomatoes
2 cups (500 ml) water
½ tsp (2 ml) dill
½ tsp (2 ml) caraway seeds
⅛ tsp (1 ml) black pepper
2-3 Tbsp (30-45 ml) sucanat (natural cane sugar)
1-2 Tbsp apple cider vinegar

Using a food processor, grate all the vegetables and place them in a pot with the stock, tomatoes, water, dill, caraway seeds and pepper.

Bring to the boil, reduce heat and simmer until the vegetables are very soft (25-40 minutes). Add in the sugar and vinegar, stir and simmer for another 5 minutes. Taste and adjust seasonings and serve. For a more elegant soup, blend before serving.

Serves 8-10

Creamy Roasted Garlic Tomato Soup

*Try and find the reddest tomatoes you can for a rich coloured soup.
The roasted garlic has a much milder flavour than raw garlic and it
contributes to the creamy outcome of the soup. This soup is also high
in the phytochemical, lycopene that has been shown to protect
against cancer, particularly prostate cancer.*

20 roasted garlic cloves (see roasted garlic on page 147)
1 large onion
3 Tbs (45 ml) olive oil
2 tsp (10 ml) fresh basil, chopped (or 1 tsp dried)
1 tsp fresh oregano, chopped (or ½ tsp dried)
4 cups (1 L) tomatoes, fresh and chopped
4 cups (1 L) water or vegetable broth
Salt and pepper to taste

In a large soup pot, sauté onion in the oil over medium heat until translucent, but
not brown. Add chopped tomato, basil and oregano and stir for one minute. Add
the stock or water, bring to a boil and then reduce the heat to low. Simmer for
about 45 minutes.

Add the roasted garlic and use a hand or immersion blender to roughly puree the
soup. Season with salt and pepper and serve.

Serves 8

Red Hot Soup

This soup is ready in 15 minutes and really packs a punch providing 189 percent of your recommended vitamin C per serving and it's also loaded with beta-carotene from the peppers, tomatoes and orange juice. Enjoy for lunches at work or a starter for dinner. Blend for a creamier tomato soup.

2 Tbsp (30 ml) olive oil
1 medium onion, chopped
4 medium garlic cloves, crushed
1 Tbsp (15 ml) ginger root (approx 1 inch), grated
1 red bell pepper, seeded and chopped
2 cups (500 ml) vegetable broth or water
1 28oz (900 g) can diced tomatoes
1 tsp (5 ml) ground coriander
¼ tsp (1 ml) ground cinnamon
¼ tsp (1 ml) cayenne pepper
2 cups (500 ml) freshly squeezed orange juice, or orange juice with pulp

Heat oil in a soup pot over medium heat. Add onions, garlic, ginger and pepper and sauté for 5-8 minutes. Add broth, tomatoes, coriander, cinnamon and cayenne. Simmer and cook for 10 minutes. Add orange juice, warm through and serve. Season to taste.

Serves 4

Speedy Tomato Basil Soup

This soup can easily be made after work, virtually no chopping is required and the soup can cook while you get changed out of your work clothes. The tomatoes provide an excellent source of lycopene, a cancer protective pigment, and the basil adds authentic Italian flavour with benefits to digestion.

2 Tbsp (30 ml) olive oil
1 onion, finely diced
1 cup (250 ml) red lentils
1 28 oz (900 g) can of crushed or diced tomatoes
4 cups (1 L) vegetable stock
Salt and Pepper to taste
2 Tbsp (30 ml) dried or fresh basil, finely chopped

In a soup pot, fry the onion in the olive oil over medium-high heat. Add the red lentils, tomatoes and stock. Cover and bring to the boil. Reduce the heat to medium-low and simmer for twenty minutes. Stir in the salt, pepper and basil and serve.

Serves 6

Signy's Medicinal Miso Soup

Signy: This is the soup I have always made when I get a cold, it comforts me, and it boosts my immune system. Because I make it for colds (when my taste buds are off) and because it is almost entirely medicinal, some of the proportions are all about getting healthy (check out how much garlic there is for instance). I encourage you to play with the proportions, so that the taste suits you.

8 cups (2 L) of water
6-7 cloves of garlic, finely chopped
1 cup (250 ml) parsley, finely chopped
1 cup (250 ml) green onion, sliced and using the green part too
1 ½ cup (375 ml) celery sliced (about 2 ribs)
200 grams firm tofu, diced up in about 1 cm cubes
½ cup (125 ml) of dried seaweed (wakame, hijiki , kombu etc) broken up into 1 cm strips (Hint: cut them with scissors)
½ cup (125 ml) onion, finely diced
1 cup (250 ml) fresh burdock root, sliced
4 cups (1 L) kale, chard or other green leafy vegetable
¾ cups (185 ml) of miso
¾ boiled (185 ml) water

Place all of the ingredients (except the miso and boiled water) in a large soup pot. Bring the soup to a boil, lower the temperature and let them simmer for about 30 minutes. Everything should be well cooked. Remove from the heat. Pour the boiled water over the miso in a bowl or pyrex cup. Whisk them together until the miso is completely dissolved and the mixture is no longer lumpy. Add this to the soup, letting the tastes mingle. You can gently heat the soup, but do not bring to a boil. When you reheat this soup for later consumption, gently heat it up, do not boil it.

Serves 8

Signy's Fortified Green Lentil Soup

Signy: A word about burdock - it is an under appreciated herb good for such things as energizing the lymphatic and immune systems, blood and liver cleansing. Look for it fresh in specialty market stores or buy it dried.

1 cup (250 ml) green lentils, soaked if possible
4 cups (1 L) water
2 Tbsp (30 ml) olive oil
1 onion, diced
2 stalks celery , diced
1 large carrot, diced
2 Tbsp (30 ml) burdock root, chopped
2 inch strip (30 ml) soaked seaweed (wakame, hijiki, kombu etc.)
6 - 8 cups (1.5 - 2 L) vegetable stock
1 clove garlic, crushed
3 bay leaves
1 tsp (5 ml) salt, add to taste
½ cup (125 ml) chopped parsley

Wash and drain the lentils. Soak for 2-3 hours if possible for quicker cooking time. Add 4 cups water. Bring to a boil on high heat. Lower heat and cook for 5 minutes. Drain. In a soup pot, heat the olive oil. Sauté onion, celery and carrot until the onion is transparent. Add stock and bring to the boil. Add lentils, garlic, bay leaves, burdock, seaweed and salt. Cook for 20 minutes or until lentils are well cooked. Adjust seasoning if necessary. Serve topped with parsley.

Serves 6-8

Red Lentil And Potato Soup

Signy: I like my soups to have protein. It's a double whammy that way. High protein and water intake - I have had a hard time getting enough liquids and it was very important during treatment to flush out the chemicals and toxins.

1 cup (250 ml) red lentils
4 cups (1 L) water
2 Tbsp (30 ml) olive oil
1 cup (250 ml) diced onions
1 tsp (5 ml) ground cumin
2 - 3 cups (500 - 750 ml) potatoes, scrubbed or peeled, and diced
1 ½ tsp (7 ml) unrefined sea salt
4 cups (1 L) vegetable stock
⅓ cup (80 ml) fresh lemon juice
¼ cup (60 ml) fresh cilantro or parsley, chopped

Wash lentils and place in a pot with 4 cups water. Bring to a boil and simmer for 20 minutes. In a soup pot, heat oil on medium heat. Sauté onion and cumin for 5-7 minutes, stirring frequently. Add potatoes and salt, cook for 5 minutes longer. Add lentils with their cooking liquid. For a thicker soup use just 2 cups of stock. Add stock and let cool for 30 minutes on low heat, stirring occasionally. Just before serving, add lemon juice and cilantro.

Serves 6-8

Sensational Salads

Spinach Salad with Walnuts and Sweet Curry Dressing

Dennis: Serve this with a quick confetti rice, as the two of them are great together. This is good enough for company.

⅓ cup (80 ml) walnuts
1 Tbsp (15 ml) sesame seeds
1 bunch fresh spinach, washed or ½ bag prewashed spinach
1 tart green apple, diced
2 green onions, thinly sliced
¼ cup (60 ml) raisins

Sweet Curry Dressing
3 Tbsp (45 ml) seasoned rice vinegar
3 Tbsp (45 ml) frozen apple juice concentrate
2 tsp (10 ml) stone ground mustard
1 tsp (5 ml) tamari soy sauce
½ tsp (2 ml) curry powder.
¼ tsp (1 ml) fresh ground black pepper

Spread walnuts and sesame seeds on a cookie sheet and bake at 375 F (180 C) for 10 minutes.

In a large salad bowl, combine the spinach with the apple, onions and raisins. Add the cooled walnuts and sesame seeds. In a separate bowl or glass jar, whisk the vinegar, fruit juice concentrate, mustard, soy sauce, curry powder and pepper together. Pour over the salad and toss to mix. Serve immediately.

Serves 4

Avocado Salad with Warm Sesame Vinaigrette

The avocado in this salad adds calories, giving you a "fuller" feeling after eating it. The sesame seeds also provide some protein and calcium. This is an excellent salad in which to add roasted walnuts or almonds, and citrus fruits go well with spinach. Spinach is very high in antioxidants and minerals and contains more beta-carotene than broccoli.

½ package of organic baby spinach leaves
1 package organic romaine lettuce
2 medium avocados

Dressing
3 Tbsp (45 ml) olive oil
2 tsp (10 ml) sesame seeds, toasted
1 Tbsp (15 ml) lemon juice
2 tsp (10 ml) seeded mustard

Wash the spinach and lettuce and tear into bite size pieces. Place in a large serving bowl. Peel and slice the avocados and place on top of the leaves. In a small skillet, lightly toast the sesame seeds on low heat, add the oil, mustard and lemon juice and stir until warm. Pour (while warm) over the salad and serve immediately.

Serves 8

Warm Mediterranean Salad

This salad is a colourful addition to the dinner table. The mushrooms and warmed vegetables add healthy carotenoids and vitamins and minerals, while the beans provide the protein. Be generous with the parsley. It is high in vitamin C, iron and calcium. Chilled leftovers also make a great lunch.

2 Tbsp (30 ml) olive oil
1 medium onion, finely chopped
1 clove garlic, crushed
1 small red pepper cut into strips
90g (3 oz) green beans
90g (2 oz) crimini mushrooms, sliced
1 Tbsp (30 ml) balsamic vinegar
1 can (14 oz) white beans or mixed beans
1 cup (250 ml) chopped fresh parsley for serving

Cook onions in oil on medium heat for 2 minutes. Add the vegetables and the remaining ingredients except for the white beans. Stir for 5 minutes. Rinse and drain the beans. Toss together with vegetables and warmed oil. Sprinkle with parsley to serve.

Serves 4-6

Amazing Mango Salad

This refreshingly light salad can be perfect for brunch or as a colourful side dish. Sesame seeds are a good source of calcium and the mangoes are packed with vitamin C for optimum health and carotenes for longevity. The avocados provide good fats for healthy skin and shiny hair.

2-3 ripe avocados, peeled and diced
1 ripe mango, peeled and diced
3 green onions, finely chopped
1 red pepper, seeded and finely chopped
1 Tbsp (15 ml) sesame seeds, lightly toasted
1 head green leaf lettuce, torn into bite size pieces

Dressing
2 Tbsp (30 ml) lime juice
2 Tbsp (30 ml) maple syrup
¼ cup (60 ml) olive oil
½ tsp (2 ml) ground cumin
2 tsp (10 ml) tamari soy sauce

Place all the salad ingredients in a salad bowl. In a jar, mix the dressing ingredients and shake. Pour the dressing over the salad and stir to coat until all pieces are lightly coated. Chill for 20 minutes before serving. Sprinkle with sesame seeds. Serve in a glass bowl or dessert dish, or on a bed of leafy greens.

Serves 4

Spring Salad Mix Sensation

The health benefits of lettuce mix are almost too long to list. Some leaves are liver cleansing, while others provide powerful carotenes and chlorophyll which help with keeping immune systems strong and also protect against disease and aging. These salad varieties are also high in vitamin C, folic acid and iron

1 4-oz bag (113 g) of organic mixed baby greens
1 4-oz bag (113 g) green romaine lettuce
1 red or orange bell pepper
½ cup each of any vegetables, cut into small bite size pieces
Cauliflower, broccoli, carrots, tomatoes, cucumber etc.
1 cup (250 ml) of a protein source, chopped into small bit size pieces
    See nuts and seed options below
Seeds: Sunflower, pumpkin or sesame seeds
Nuts: almonds, walnuts or pecans Beans: seasoned tofu cubes,
    garbanzo or white beans
1 cup (250 ml) cooked whole grains (bulghar wheat, brown rice,
    barley, millet or quinoa)

Rinse the lettuce and greens with cold water and drain. Place in a large salad bowl. Chop vegetables, peppers and your chosen protein source and add to the greens in the bowl. This salad can then be placed on top of the grains on a large platter or on individual serving plates. Top with dressing of your choice or honey mustard dressing.

Left over grains are perfect for these kinds of salad and add complex carbohydrates for sustained energy, they also reduce the need for bread rolls and croutons.

Serves 12

Honey Mustard Dressing

2 Tbsp (30 ml) olive oil
2 Tbsp (30 ml) of Natural Mayonnaise or Nayonnaise
1 Tbsp (15 ml) lemon juice
1 tsp (5 ml) good quality mustard
½ tsp curry powder
½ tsp honey or natural sweetener
Salt and pepper to taste

Add all ingredients to a jar and shake to blend well.

Serves 4

Caribbean Sweet Potato Salad

Stretch out summer just a little bit longer with this refreshing tangy mix of lime and cilantro. Perfect as a side salad, or even for lunch, this is one of the tastiest ways I've found to eat yams and sweet potatoes. This recipe turns out well whether you chop the potatoes fine or in larger chunks.

1 large russet potato, peeled and chopped into 1 inch pieces
1 large sweet potato or yam, peeled and chopped into 1 inch pieces
1 cup (250 ml) corn
1 cucumber, cubed
½ red onion, thinly sliced
¼ cup (60 ml) peanuts, finely chopped

Dressing
1 tsp (5 ml) good quality mustard
2 Tbsp (30 ml) lime juice
2 Tbsp (30 ml) fresh cilantro, chopped
1 clove garlic, minced
3 Tbsp (45 ml) olive oil
½ tsp (2 ml) sea salt
¼ tsp (1 ml) ground black pepper

Bring a large pot of water to the boil and add a pinch of salt. Carefully add potatoes. Bring to the boil again and then reduce heat to simmer for 10 minutes. Add the sweet potato or yam and cook about 10 minutes more.

While potatoes are cooking, chop cucumber and onion and make the dressing. Mix mustard, lime juice, cilantro garlic, salt pepper and oil and shake in a jar. Check potatoes with a fork or knife to see that they are soft in the middle. Rinse and drain under cold water.

In a bowl, add the corn, cucumber and onion to the potatoes. Add the dressing and stir through the salad. Garnish with peanuts and serve.

Serves 6

Dandelion Greens Salad with Navy Beans

A sensational spring recipe for these strongly flavoured greens. Feel free to add more sun-dried tomatoes, and use a little of their oil for a natural tasty dressing. The tomatoes are an excellent source of lycopene and the beans add a serving of protein. This dish is also excellent served on top of baked or mashed potatoes.

8 cups (2 L) vegetable stock or water
1 medium onion
4 cloves garlic, minced
2 pounds (1kg) dandelion greens
3 sun-dried tomatoes, packed in olive oil
2 cups (500ml) cooked navy beans (if unavailable use sunflower seeds)

In a large soup pot, bring the stock or water to a boil. Trim, wash and chop the dandelion greens. Add the greens and the whole onion to the pot and simmer, uncovered, for 10 to 15 minutes, or until the greens are tender, drain. Allow to cool. Remove and discard the onion. Mince the garlic. Chop the tomatoes. Toss the greens with the garlic, tomatoes and beans. Serve hot or at room temperature.

Serves 6

Flax Oil and Raw Garlic Salad Dressing

This sensational dressing is based on the Mediterranean formula of olive oil and lemon juice. Using flax oil instead provides essential fatty acids and cancer-fighting potential. The garlic adds an additional boost. Since garlic has health benefits when both raw and cooked, this is a great way to get some raw garlic into your diet.

4 Tbsp (60 ml) flax seed oil
2 Tbsp (30 ml) nutritional yeast
2 Tbsp (60 ml) fresh lemon juice
2 garlic cloves, minced finely

In a salad dressing jar, mix all ingredients and shake well. Use on green salads, on grains, or over steamed vegetables. Keeps refrigerated for two to three days.

Serves 4

Pure Medicine Salad

Signy: Ah, the leafy green salad. My body craves this during the warmer months and it is so darn good for us! This recipe is pure medicine, let food be your medicine and medicine be your food! That is my philosophy. I like the avocado for all of the nutrients, and protein... and fats (good fats), during chemotherapy, it was good to have extra fats.

Salad
1 package mixed salad greens
Healing herbs such as chickweed, dandelion greens or wild violet leaves (violata odorata)
½ cup (125 ml) parsley, chopped
½ cup (125 ml) sunflower seeds
½ cup (125 ml) sprouted lentils or bean sprouts
1 or 2 ripe avocados, sliced or cubed

Dressing
2 Tbsp (30 ml) flax seed oil
1 Tbsp (15 ml) olive oil
2 tsp (5 ml) Braggs or Tamari soy sauce
¾ Tbsp (10 ml) freshly squeezed lemon juice
1 clove garlic, minced
1½ Tbsp (22 ml) ground flax seeds

In the bottom of the salad bowl, whisk the flax oil, olive oil, Braggs, lemon juice and garlic until they have a nice consistency, it should get opaque. Check the taste and adjust the lemon juice to taste. Right before you plan to throw the greens into the bowl add the ground flax seeds. Whisk that all together. Add the salad greens and any healing herbs plus the sunflower seeds, parsley and lentils. Toss until well coated with dressing.
Add the avocado and stir gently, being careful not to let it get mushy.

Serves 4

Thai Noodle Salad

Signy: I tried this salad specifically because it calls for burdock root. So good for us!

225 g (approx. ½ lb.) buckwheat, rice, or yam noodles
½ cup (125 ml) dry hiziki seaweed

Marinade
¼ cup (60 ml) tamari soy sauce or Braggs aminos
1½ lemons, juiced
1 tsp (5 ml) ginger, grated
1 tsp (5 ml) garlic, crushed
½ cup (125 ml) water
¼ tsp (1 ml) cayenne, optional

200g (approx ½ lb.) firm tofu, sliced into thin julienne strips.

Vegetables
1 stalk celery, thin diagonal slices
1 medium carrot, thin diagonal slices
2 cups (500 ml) burdock root, scraped or scrubbed, thin diagonal slices
1 bunch green onions, thin diagonal slices
1 large red pepper, sliced
1 large green pepper, sliced
2 cups (500 ml) finely chopped parsley
½ cup (125 ml) thinly sliced red cabbage

½ cup (125 ml) natural smooth peanut butter

Cook noodles according to directions on package, then drain and cool.
Soak hiziki in 2 cups water for 1 hour. Drain and thoroughly squeeze out excess liquid.

Combine the marinade ingredients, except tofu in a bowl, mixing thoroughly. Place tofu in the mixture and marinate for 1 hour. Remove tofu and drain, reserving the liquid.

Combine noodles, marinated tofu, seaweed and vegetables in a very large bowl. Place smooth peanut butter and marinade liquid from above in a blender. Process until smooth. Taste, adding more ginger and garlic if necessary. Pour over salad and mix.

Serves 10-12

Amazing Grain Salads

Perfectly Fluffy Grains

Dennis: Make sure you double the rice recipe, so you can use it again during the week for any grain salad recipe.

4 cups water
1 cup grain
½ tsp sea salt

Boil the water (yes it is meant to be 4 cups). Add the sea salt. Add the grains, cover and simmer, for the recommended cooking time (page 68). Do not lift lid, or stir, until the time has passed. Rinse the cooked grain under hot water to make it fluffier, and drain. Make the rice the night before and store in refrigerator, covered, after it cools. To cool quickly for immediate use, run the grain under cold water in a colander or strainer.

Makes 2-3 cups rice

Mexican Grain Salad

There's no need to cook grains every night. One batch of brown rice can be cooked one evening and then cooled and refrigerated for 2-3 days. Then it can be re-heated or used in this recipe as an easy dinner or side salad. Just chop some veggies, open the beans and mix it all together with some salsa. Ole!

1 cup (250 ml) short or long grain organic brown rice
4 cups (1 L) water
½ tsp (2 ml) salt

1 14-oz (454 ml) can black or kidney beans
1 cup (250ml) each of chopped green and red peppers, green onion, and corn kernels
1-2 cups (250-500 ml) sugar-free salsa
½ cup (125 ml) chopped cilantro

For the rice, follow the Perfectly Fluffy Grains recipe (page 115).
Drain beans and add to rice along with chopped vegetables and cilantro. Add salsa. Stir together, and eat immediately or serve in small containers for grabbing throughout the week for lunch.

Serves 8

Mediterranean Wild Rice Salad with Chickpeas

This hearty salad welcomes all new patients at the Centre for Integrated Healing when it is served at the Introductory Program. A tasty introduction to the way of whole foods eating, it is served with a spinach salad and hummus. It provides complex carbohydrates, protein and healthy fats all in one hit.

¾ cup (185 ml) brown rice, long grain
¼ cup (60 ml) wild rice
3 tomatoes, chopped
1 cucumber, chopped
1 cup (250 ml) parsley, chopped
1 14 oz can chick peas
¼ cup (60 ml) fresh herbs (basil, oregano, etc. if available)

Dressing:
2 cloves garlic, chopped
¼ cup (60 ml) olive oil
¼ cup (60 ml) lemon juice
1 tsp (5 ml) salt

Bring 4 cups of water to the boil in a large pot. When boiling add a pinch of salt. Add the brown and wild rice. Cover and turn the heat down to low. Cook for 45 minutes. Do not uncover. Do not stir. Drain the cooked rice and rinse under cold water.

Add the chopped vegetables, herbs and chickpeas. Stir gently to mix.

In a separate bowl or jar, mix the dressing ingredients. Mix well, pour on salad and stir through.

Serves 6

Quick Confetti Rice

Dennis: This is a wonderful coloured rice pilaf, and with the spinach salad it has great eye appeal and a sensational taste. It is a real winner.

2 Tbsp (30 ml) water or vegetable stock
2 cups (500 ml) cooked brown basmati rice
½ cup (125 ml) frozen or fresh corn
½ cup (125 ml) frozen or fresh peas
½ red bell pepper, diced
½ tsp (7 ml) curry powder
½ cup (60 ml) raisins
Sea salt

Heat the water or vegetable stock in a large nonstick skillet. Add the cooked rice, then use a spatula or the back of a wooden spoon to separate the rice. Add corn, peas, red bell pepper pieces, curry powder and raisins. Heat thoroughly. Add salt if needed.

Makes 3 cups

Ancient Grain Salad

This salad is a consistent hit for potlucks and parties, or enjoy it all by yourself for a fully satisfying lunch. The mushrooms add protein and a meaty texture. I love it because it's perfect for using up any vegetables left in the fridge at the end of the week.

1 cup (250 ml) quinoa, kamut or millet
½ cup (125 ml) toasted sunflower seeds
1½ cups (385 ml) shiitake mushrooms, sliced
2 tsp (10 ml) sea salt
¼ cup (60 ml) red onion or scallions, chopped
Add approximately ½ cup of any or all of the following:
carrots, any color bell pepper, sprouts, cabbage, cucumber, tomato, lettuce

Italian Dressing
2 cloves garlic, minced
⅓ cup (85 ml) red wine vinegar
1 Tbsp (15 ml) balsamic vinegar
3 Tbsp (45 ml) fresh flax oil
1 tsp (5 ml) Italian seasonings
1 tsp (5 ml) sea salt

Cook the grains and let cool in a large bowl (or run them under cold water and drain). Fry the mushrooms in a skillet with a bit of water in the bottom until tender, about 5 to 10 minutes. Drain the mushrooms and add, along with the rest of the salad ingredients, to the cooked grains.

Drizzle with Italian dressing and lightly toss. (Dressing Instructions: mix all ingredients and shake in a jar.)

Serves 6

Barley Salad with Tomatoes and Corn

Dennis: This is a great recipe for company or a `pot luck. This is one of my favourites, any time of year. This recipe came from my organic delivery company.

1 cup (250 ml) pearl barley
2½ cups (625 ml) water
1 pint cherry tomatoes
2 cups (500 ml) corn kernels, fresh or frozen
¼ cup (60 ml) diced red onion
1 cup (250 ml) crumbled extra firm tofu (optional)

Dressing
1 cup (250 ml) fresh basil, chopped
⅓ cup (80 ml) nutritional yeast (optional)
¼ cup (60 ml) olive oil
2 Tbsp (30 ml) balsamic vinegar
2 cloves garlic

Bring 2½ cups water to a boil. Add the barley and simmer, covered, for 40 minutes.

Drain and rinse with cold water. While barley is cooking, whisk together olive oil, vinegar, basil, nutritional yeast, and garlic to make the dressing. Toss barley, corn, tomatoes, onion, and tofu, together with dressing. Season with salt and pepper and garnish with additional basil leaves.

Serves 6

Italian Fasta Pasta Salad

Having these staples on hand makes for a quick salad that can be enhanced by fresh tomatoes and herbs. These, of course add valuable vitamins and plant nutrients such as vitamin C and E , chlorophyll and lycopene. Try adding 1-2 tablespoons of fresh chopped basil, oregano or parsley...or all three!

250 g whole grain pasta (such as kamut pasta)
5 Tbsp (75 ml) pre-made pesto (available in jars in the supermarket)
1 cup (250 ml) cherry tomatoes
½ cup (125 ml) kalamata olives (available in jars in the supermarket)
Fresh herbs, finely chopped when available

Cook the pasta as directed on the package. Drain and rinse with warm water. Place in a large salad bowl. Stir the pesto through the pasta until the pasta is well coated. Add the tomatoes, olives and herbs. Mix well. Serve at room temperature. This salad is ideal as left-overs for lunch.

Serves 4-6

Brown Rice Salad with Tahini Sauce

Brad: Here are a couple of original fixin's my wife, Lenore, and I have come up with over the years.

2 cups (500 ml) hot cooked brown rice
2 cups (500 ml) spinach leaves, washed
½ cup (125 ml) bean sprouts of your choice
½ cup (125 ml) carrot, grated
½ cup (125 ml) raw beets, grated
½ cup (125 ml) red peppers, diced
1 dozen green beans, steamed but still crunchy
4 Tbsp (60 ml) sesame seeds, lightly toasted
½ cup (125 ml) tahini sauce (see below)

Divide the ingredients evenly between two separate bowls. On a bed of the hot rice place the spinach and other fresh ingredients. Pour on tahini sauce and top with sesame seeds

Serves 2

Tahini Sauce

Brad: A perfect topping for salads, cooked grains or vegetables.

½ cup (125 ml) tahini
1 Tbsp (15 ml) fresh lemon juice
1 garlic clove, finely chopped OR 1 Tbsp (15 ml) finely chopped onion
Sea salt to taste
Hot water, to thin to a sauce consistency

Combine the tahini, lemon juice and garlic or onion in a small pot and heat until nearly hot. (Or place in a measuring cup and heat in microwave). Add hot water to bring to an easily poured sauce consistency and add salt to taste.
Makes ¾ cup

Brown Rice and Black Bean Hash

Brad: Another comfort food, simple, filling and delicious.

1 cup (250 ml) uncooked brown rice
1 cup (250 ml) crumbled feta cheese
1 14 oz can (454 ml) black beans, drained and rinsed
1 can (454 ml) nibblets style sweet corn, drained
½ cup (125 ml) black olives, sliced
½ cup (125 ml) cilantro, chopped
2 fresh tomatoes, diced

Cook rice as per grain cooking instructions (page 115). Add all ingredients to hot cooked rice, except the tomatoes, and stir in. Serve in bowls and top with fresh tomatoes. Add sea salt to taste.

Serves 4

Indonesian Grain Salad

This salad has all the nutrients of a full meal. The nuts and seeds give protein while the rice gives sustained energy in the form of complex carbohydrates. Fruits and vegetables are also featured for maximum cancer-fighting value.

2 cups (500ml) cooked brown rice
½ cup (125 ml) raisins
2 green onions, chopped
½ cup (125 ml) sesame seeds, toasted
½ cup (125 ml) cashews, toasted
1 cup (250 ml) water chestnuts, sliced
1 green pepper, diced
1 red pepper, diced

Asian Dressing
½ cup (125 ml) parsley, chopped
¾ cup (185 ml) orange or pineapple juice
¼ cup (60ml) cold pressed olive oil
1 Tbsp (15 ml) cold pressed sesame oil
1 lemon, juiced and chopped peel
4 Tbsp (60 ml) tamari soy sauce

Shake the dressing ingredients in a jar. Combine the rice, seeds, nuts and vegetables in a large bowl. Add the dressing. Chill before serving.

Serves 6

Tabouleh

This classic Middle Eastern Salad is so refreshing when made with fresh herbs. If mint is not available, use any fresh herbs you have. The parsley is high in calcium, iron and chlorophyll, the grains give you extended energy and B vitamins to help with stress.

1 cup (250 ml) bulghar or kibbled wheat
3 cups (750 ml) boiling water
¼ cup (60 ml) green onions, chopped
1 cup (250 ml) parsley, chopped
½ cup (125 ml) mint, chopped
1-2 cups tomato, finely cubed

Basic Mediterranean Dressing:
¼ cup (60 ml) lemon juice
¼ cup (60 ml) olive oil
Sea salt and pepper to taste

In a large bowl, pour the boiling water over the bulghar and let sit for 20 minutes. When the grain is soft, rinse under cold water using a colander or wire-mesh sieve and let drain. While the bulghar is soaking, blend the dressing ingredients together in a jar and chop the onions, parsley, mint and tomato. Put the drained wheat mixture in a bowl with the vegetables and dressing. Toss to mix, and season carefully using enough salt to bring out the flavours.

Serve in a bowl lined with lettuce leaves.

Note:If you are making this salad several hours before it is to be eaten, stir the tomato into it in the last half hour so the tomato does not make the wheat soggy. You can also make the salad with precooked brown rice, kamut or barley.

Alter proportions to suit your taste or make additions such as chopped red or green peppers, olives, celery, cucumber, radishes, garlic, etc.

Serves 4

Beet and Barley Salad with Toasted Walnuts

Grain salads such as this one are perfect for combining vegetables with something other than rice, bread or potatoes. The beets provide loads of vitamin C and beta-carotene and add a wonderful colourful element to any meal. Serve this salad on some kale or any large leafy greens.

1 cup (250 ml) pearl barley
1 tsp (5 ml) sea salt
8 small beets
¼ cup (60 ml) red wine vinegar
3 cloves garlic, minced
1 Tbsp (15 ml) Dijon mustard
¼ tsp (1 ml) each salt and pepper
¼ cup (60 ml) olive oil
¼ cup (85 ml) cold pressed walnut oil
1 cup (250 ml) chopped fresh walnuts, toasted

6 cups torn arugula, asian salad mix or mixed salad greens

Bring 4 cups of water to the boil in a large pot. Add 1 tsp sea salt and barley. Place lid on pot, reduce heat to low and leave to cook for 40 minutes.

Wash and scrub beets and slice or dice them in ¼ inch slices or 1 cm cubes.

Place beets to cook in a steamer over boiling water, for around 20 minutes, until they are tender. Test they are firm but soft with a sharp knife.

Whisk together the vinegar, garlic, mustard and salt and pepper in small bowl. Gradually whisk in olive oil and walnut oil.

Add ¼ cup of dressing to warm beets, toss and let cool.

When barley is soft, remove from heat, rinse with cold water and drain. Fluff with a fork and toss in remaining dressing.

Add walnuts and greens to the barley. Spread on a large serving platter.

Top the barley with the beets and drizzle with any remaining dressing.

Serves 8

Tasty Entrees and Vegetables

Amazing Pasta Sauce

Pat: Another easy favourite, I sometimes sprinkle Italian spice, garlic powder, low sodium soy sauce or grated goat's cheese on top, before serving with brown rice or cubed toast and a salad. This mix is useful for, shepherd's pie and stuffing peppers.

2 Tbsp (30 ml) olive oil
3 Tbsp (45 ml) water
2 or 3 organic sweet peppers, any colour, diced
1 large organic onion, diced
6 garlic cloves, chopped
1 package Yves Veggie Ground Round Original, chopped finely

Using a large fry pan or skillet add olive oil and water. Add the chopped peppers, onion and garlic. Cook at high heat for 2 minutes, stirring constantly and then turn heat down and cover for about 3 minutes, until not yet mushy.

Remove from stove and add Yves Veggie Ground Round Original. (This is already cooked so it only needs to be heated a short time when the fry pan is returned to the stove.)

Serves 2

Mel's Tex-Mex Tamale Pie

Mel: This recipe added to our adventures with soy. I loved it! I enjoyed the texture of the "ground round" and all the tex-mex flavours.

1 Tbsp (15 ml) olive oil
¾ lb (350 g) Yves Veggie Ground Round
1 medium onion, chopped
1 can (454 ml) whole kernel corn, with liquid
1 can (454 ml) chopped tomatoes
1 cup (250 ml) sour cream (or 250 g soft tofu mixed with ¼ tsp garlic salt and 1 tsp lemon juice)
1 cup (250 ml) corn meal
1 small can (125 ml) olives, sliced
1 Tbsp (15 ml) chili powder
1 tsp (5 ml) sea salt
½ tsp (2 ml) ground cumin
1 cup (250 ml) monterey jack cheese (organic or soy version)
Salsa

In a heavy, 25 cm or 10-inch oven-proof pan, heat oil and cook onions and the veggie ground round. Sauté for 5 minutes. Stir in the remaining ingredients corn, tomatoes, sour cream/tofu, cornmeal, olives, chili powder, sea salt and cumin. Mix well, cover, reduce heat to low and simmer for 20 minutes. The mixture will have a thick pie-like consistency. Sprinkle with cheese and broil in the oven until golden, just 3 minutes. Serve with salsa and green leafy salad.

Serves 6

Stir-Fried Tofu with Broccoli

Mel: We have used soy products for a long time but after the cancer we use it even more. We feel it is healthy and helpful. This recipe is convenient because you can substitute a variety of vegetables. Our three kids all love it too.

450 g firm or extra-firm tofu, cut into 1 inch cubes
2 Tbsp (30 ml) olive oil
2 Tbsp (30 ml) ginger root, chopped finely
2 onions, sliced
6 cups (1.5 L) broccoli, chopped
1 cup (250 ml) carrots, thinly sliced
½ lb (250 ml) Asian mushrooms, sliced
¾ cup (185 ml) vegetable stock
2 tsp (10 ml) tamari soy sauce
2 tsp (10 ml) cornstarch (Preferred: ground arrowroot)
2 Tbsp (30 ml) water
4 cups (1 L) Chinese cabbage or bok choy, sliced

In a wok, over high heat, heat the oil and add the tofu with half of the ginger root. Stir-fry together for 2 minutes. Remove the tofu and ginger from the wok, set aside in a bowl. Add the onions to the wok, stir-fry for 2 minutes and then add to the tofu in the bowl. With the remaining ginger root, add the broccoli, carrots and mushrooms and stir-fry for 2 minutes. Add the vegetable stock and soy sauce to the broccoli, stir, cover and cook for 2 more minutes. In a separate bowl, mix the arrowroot and water together. Add the tofu and onion back to the vegetables in the wok and add the arrowroot mixture, bringing to the boil. Stir in the cabbage or bok-choy and cook until tender but crisp (1 minute). Serve over whole grains.

Serves 6

Even Easier Stir-Fry

Mel: Fresh vegetables are so important. This recipe allowed me to get lots of them. It's easy to eat and digest and very healthy. We added tofu to the original recipe idea.

1 Tbsp (15 ml) olive oil
450 g firm or extra-firm tofu, cut into 1-cm cubes
2 cups (500 ml) cauliflower, cut into bite size pieces
2 cups (500 ml) broccoli, cut into bite size pieces
4 medium carrots, sliced
½ cup (125 ml) vegetable stock
¼ lb (125 g) snow peas
1 tsp (5 ml) garlic, finely chopped
2 Tbsp (30 ml) ginger root, grated
4 cups (1 L) red or green cabbage, chopped
1 Tbsp (15 ml) soy sauce

In a wok, over medium-high heat, heat oil and add cauliflower, broccoli and carrots. Stir-fry for 3 minutes. Add in the vegetable stock, cover and steam for 2 minutes. Add the snow peas and tofu stir well and cook for another minute. Add the garlic, ginger root and cabbage, cook until tender but crisp. Stir in soy sauce and serve on whole grains.

Serves 6

Best Ever Bean Chili

Dennis: People tell me that this is the best chili they have ever tasted, and I agree!

1 14-oz (454 ml) can kidney beans - drained and rinsed
1 14-oz (454 ml) can garbanzo beans - drained and rinsed
1 onion, diced
1 large carrot, diced
1 large stalk of celery, diced
1 cup (250 ml) mushrooms, sliced
½ green pepper, sliced
2 garlic cloves, minced
¾ cup (185 ml) tomato paste
2 large tomatoes, diced
1 tsp (5 ml) ground cumin
1½ tsp (7 ml) chili powder
1½ tsp (2 ml) pepper
¼ tsp (1 ml) sea salt
1 package Yves Ground Round Original (optional)

Sauté all the vegetables in a large lightly oiled skillet until onion is transparent. Add tomato paste, tomatoes, beans and seasonings. Simmer, covered, 40 minutes, adding water to keep moist. If using Yves Ground Round, add after 35 minutes and heat thoroughly for 5 minutes.

Serves 8

Peanut Stew

This easy soup has a delightfully complex flavour. The yams are an excellent complex carbohydrate for staying warm through the winter and provide beta-carotene and vitamin C in large amounts. The chickpeas are an easily digested protein and almond butter can be used instead of peanut butter to add more calcium.

3 Tbsp (30 ml) soy sauce
1 onion, sliced
2 cups (500ml) yams, peeled and diced in 1-inch cubes
1 carrot, sliced
1 celery stalk, sliced
1 red bell pepper, diced
4 cups (1 L) vegetable stock
1 15 oz (465 g) can garbanzo beans
1 15 oz (465 g) can crushed tomatoes
½ cup (125 ml) fresh cilantro, chopped
⅓ cup (80 ml) natural peanut butter
2 tsp (10 ml) curry powder

Heat ½ cup (125 ml) of water and the soy sauce in a large pot. Add onion and yams. Cook over high heat, stirring occasionally, for 5 minutes. Add carrot, celery, and pepper. Cover and cook 5 minutes, stirring occasionally. Add tomatoes, stock, garbanzo beans, and cilantro. Blend peanut butter with ⅓ cup (80 ml) of water then add it to the soup along with curry powder. Stir, then cover and simmer 10 minutes.

This soup freezes well. Serve with cooked grains and a green salad.

Serves 8-10

Mushroom Gravy

Anything tastes good when smothered in gravy. The perfect winter comfort food. The mushrooms add important B vitamins that help to reduce stress and this recipe is low in fat! Why not try the leftovers on home-made oven-baked fries?

1 Tbsp (15 ml) tamari soy sauce
1 cup finely chopped onion
2 cups sliced crimini mushrooms (or any Asian mushroom with a brown skin), finely sliced
2 Tbsp (30ml) whole wheat pastry flour
½ tsp (2ml) garlic granules or powder
¼ tsp (1ml) poultry seasoning
¼ tsp (1ml) sea salt
¼ tsp (1ml) fresh ground black pepper

Heat ½ cup water and the soy sauce in a fry pan or large pot. Add the onions and mushrooms. Cover and cook on med-high heat for about 10 minutes, stirring often. Mix the flour with 2 cups of hot water and add it to the cooked onion mixture. Add the seasonings. With a whisk, stir constantly over medium heat until thick. (Do not answer the door or phone at this point...the gravy must be stirred!) For a smoother gravy, blend using a blender or hand-immersion blender.

Makes about 1½ cups (375ml)

Walnut Lentil Loaf

This festive loaf can be turned out and dressed up with a holly and berry garnish for the Holidays. Decorating with natural greenery around the serving dish also highlights the warm mushroom colour. Perfect for vegetarians and meat-lovers alike, make sure you make enough for everyone.

¾ cup (185ml) brown lentils
½ cup (125 ml) water
2 Tbsp (30ml) apple cider vinegar
1 Tbsp (15ml) sesame or olive oil
1 cup (250 ml) finely minced onion
5 large cloves of garlic, minced
½ cup (125ml) finely ground walnuts
1 tsp (5ml) sea salt
2 cups (500 ml) fresh spinach, finely sliced
1 tsp (5ml) seeded or good-quality mustard
Fresh ground black pepper to taste
½ cup (125ml) fine whole wheat bread crumbs or fresh wheat germ

Bring the lentils and water to a boil. Lower heat to med-low and simmer, partially covered for 30 minutes or until the lentils are "mushy" and the water has disappeared. Transfer to a medium sized bowl, add vinegar and mash well.

Heat the oil in a pan over medium heat, sauté the onions for 5 minutes and add the garlic, nuts , seasonings and spinach. Saute for another five to ten minutes until all the vegetables are tender. Add the bread crumbs and the sautéd vegetables to the lentil mixture.

Mix well and spoon into a lightly oiled pan. Press down gently with a spatula. Bake at 350 F (180 C) for about 40 minutes. Let cool for 5-10 minutes before removing from the loaf pan.

Garnish and serve with gravy.

Serves 6-10

Slow Roasted Vegetables

The slow cooking of the vegetables really brings out their sweetness, but if you need to have the meal ready faster then steam all the vegetables for about 10 minutes before placing them in the oven. The peppers and yellow onions add further sweetness. This recipe is an excellent side-dish or works well as left-overs.

2 potatoes, cut into rough 1-inch cubes (leave skins on)
2 small eggplants, cut into 1-inch slices
2 yellow (or white) onions, quartered
2-4 red bell peppers, seeded and quartered
1 zucchini cut sliced, and slices cut into quarters
¼ cup (60ml) olive oil

Dressing
⅔ cup (165ml) olive oil
4 cloves garlic, peeled and crushed
1 cup (250ml) fresh basil, tear leaves into small pieces

Preheat oven to 400 F. In a casserole dish or a tin-foil package place all the vegetables. Drizzle with one quarter cup of olive oil and toss lightly. Cover and place in the oven for 50 minutes.

When all pieces are soft, remove the vegetables and add them to the dressing. Toss until well coated. Serve warm or at room temperature. Can also be served on crusty whole-grain bread or grains.

Serves 6

Ratatouille Pizza

Using a pre-made whole wheat pizza crust can make this recipe even easier. If that's not available, bread machines can make up a great dough. The eggplant, zucchini, tomatoes and Italian seasonings make this a family favourite that can be "built" with the help of little hands too!

1 pizza crust
1 small eggplant, thinly sliced
1 small zucchini, thinly sliced
1 medium bell pepper
½ small red onion
2 Tbsp (30 ml) olive oil
½ cup (125 ml) canned diced tomatoes
2 cloves garlic, minced
1 tsp (5 ml) dried thyme leaves or 1 Tbsp fresh thyme
Salt and pepper, to taste
½ cup (125 ml) grated mozzarella or Soy equivalent
Extra olive oil

Preheat oven to 400 F (200 C). Prepare dough or pizza crust and set it aside to rest.

Slice eggplant, zucchini, bell pepper, and onion using your processor's thinnest slicing blade. Toss with ½ of the oil and set aside.

Lightly spray or oil a baking sheet. Transfer dough to prepared baking sheet. Spread remaining oil over dough and top with tomatoes. Sprinkle with garlic, and thyme. Arrange eggplant, zucchini, pepper, and onion slices over top. Sprinkle with salt, pepper, and mozzarella. Bake for about 20 minutes, until cheese is bubbly and crust is golden. For pre-baked pizza bases, bake for 12 -18 minutes. Remove pizza from oven and slide from sheet onto a rack to cool for 5 minutes. Slice and enjoy.

Serves 4

Veggie Bake

Signy: This bake is delicious with fish, or if I don't want to have it with salmon I will add tofu or tempeh to the veggies while they are cooking.

1 onion, quartered
¼ cup (60 ml) water
1 cup (250 ml) yam
1 cup (250 ml) carrot
1 cup (250 ml) turnip
1 cup (250 ml) butternut squash (my favourite is butternut as it's easiest to cut up)
1 cup (250 ml) beet
300 grams firm or extra-firm tofu (optional)
¼-½ cup (60-125 ml) olive oil
Spices to taste (rosemary, oregano, basil for example)
1-2 tsp (5-10 ml) sea salt

Heat oven to 400 F (200 C). Wash and cut all vegetables into 1 inch cubes. Using a large baking dish with lid, add the onions and water, and then the vegetables that take longest to cook, beets, turnips and carrot. Add the tofu if using. Then add the squash and yam. Drizzle with olive oil, add spices and mix lightly.

Bake for 45-50 minutes and serve with grains, salad or soup.

Serves 4

Eggplant and Tomato Casserole

This unassuming dish is absolutely delicious, and after trying it just once, you'll always know what to do with eggplant. There's something about the eggplant that gives this dish a real "meaty" texture and makes it a favourite among new vegetarians. Eggplant lowers blood cholesterol and improves digestion.

1 large eggplant, cut into 1-cm slices
¼ cup (60 ml) olive oil
½ cup (125 ml) whole wheat bread crumbs

2 onions, quartered and sliced
2 Tbsp (30 ml) water
8 large tomatoes, sliced
1 Tbsp (15 ml) fresh basil or 1 tsp (5 ml) dried
½ cup (125 ml) water
1 tsp (5 ml) salt
1 tsp (5 ml) natural sugar
1 tsp (5 ml) pepper
½ cup (125 ml) soy cheese, grated

Preheat the oven to 350 F (180 C). Place the bread crumbs in a broad shallow dish. Coat the eggplant slices with a little olive oil and dip into the breadcrumbs to coat. Brown the coated slices lightly in a fry pan. While the eggplant is browning, cook the onions with the 2 Tbsp of water in a large pot on medium heat, for 5 minutes. Add the tomato slices, water, salt, sugar and basil. Simmer until the onion is tender.

Place the browned eggplant slices in a large casserole dish, cutting them to fit if necessary. Pour some of the tomato mixture over the eggplant to cover them. Repeat if necessary. Top with the grated cheese and ground black pepper. Bake, uncovered, for 40 minutes or until the top browns and the eggplant is very tender. Cool for 10 minutes before serving. Ideally served with other vegetables, salad or grains.

Serves 4

Walnut and Four Greens Sauté

These greens pack a powerful load of antioxidants and liver-cleansing potential. All of the greens are interchangeable, so don't worry if you don't have them all. This recipe is also flexible for using in the fall. The garlic adds an immune-boosting and flavourful punch and the walnuts provide essential fats.

1 bunch (½ pound) 250g beet greens or kale
1 bunch (½ pound) 250g collards
1 bunch (½ pound) 250g dandelion greens
1 bunch (½ pound) 250g mustard greens
1 Tbsp (15 ml) olive oil
4 cloves garlic, minced
Sea salt to taste
½ cup (125 ml) walnut pieces

Toast the walnuts in a 350 F (180 C) oven for 10 minutes.

Wash and chop the greens. Boil the greens in 4 cups (1000 ml) of water for 10 minutes, covered. Cook until soft. In a large skillet, heat the oil over medium heat. Add the garlic and sauté briefly. Add the greens and continue to sauté for 5 minutes. Add a pinch of salt, to taste. Add the walnut pieces. Serve immediately. These are ideal with mashed potato.

Serves 8

Grilled Kebobs

These delicious kabobs are a tasty high protein option at any barbeque. Mixed with colourful vegetables, you get maximum antioxidant intake too. Both the ginger and sesame oil featured in the marinade have anti-aging properties. They are also critical for the flavour of the tofu. Be sure to marinate for over an hour.

Marinade:
2 Tbsp (30 ml) tamari soy sauce
1 Tbsp (15 ml) expeller pressed toasted sesame oil
1 Tbsp (15 ml) fresh ginger, finely grated
2 cloves garlic, crushed

1 lb (500 g) extra-firm tofu
½ Spanish onion, cut into 1-inch cubes
16 medium sized crimini mushrooms, cleaned
1 large green pepper, cut into 1-inch cubes
1 large red pepper, cut into 1-inch cubes
1 Tbsp (15 ml) olive oil as needed

In a large bowl or flat dish mix the marinade ingredients. Cut tofu into 1 and ½ inch cubes, place in marinade, cover and marinate for at least an hour or more. (Marinate in the fridge for longer than 2 hours)

Steam the onions for 3-4 minutes until they become tender. Alternately thread marinated tofu and vegetables onto skewers. Brush the kebobs with oil and place on the bottom rack of the grill. Cook over low heat, turning often for about 10 minutes or until tofu is grilled. Serve over a bed of grains with barbeque sauce and a salad.

Serves 4

Marinated Grilled Vegetables

This Mediterranean-based dish is easy and versatile. It can be done with just one or all of the vegetables for an incredibly tasty side dish or entree served on grains with salad. This is a sure way to get carotenes, bioflavanoids, and the health benefits of olive oil and garlic into your menu.

Marinade
2 Tbsp (30 ml) olive oil
2 Tbsp (30 ml) balsamic vinegar
1 tsp (5 ml) herbs de Provence
2 cloves garlic, pressed

4 portobella or portobello mushrooms, thickly sliced
1 eggplant, thickly sliced
2 zucchini, thickly sliced
2 coloured bell peppers, thickly sliced
1 red onion, thickly sliced

In a large bowl mix the marinade. Toss the sliced vegetables in the marinade until well covered. Place the vegetables directly on the hot grill or use a grilling basket. Grill until marks appear on the vegetables. Turn over and cook until softened. Serve hot, at room temperature or chilled.

Serves 6

Greens with Wild Mushrooms and Garlic

Eating greens has never been a problem for me since I started combining them with the powerful flavours of garlic, ginger and the creamy texture of mushrooms. Use fresh wild mushrooms, or re-hydrate the dried mushrooms found all year round in the produce department of your supermarket. Shiitake mushrooms, while more expensive, provide an extra immune boost.

2 bunches (2 kg) of kale, chard, collard greens, spinach or a combination of each
1-2 cups (250 - 500 ml) wild mushrooms, sliced (oyster, portobello, shiitake, crimini or other)
2-4 large cloves of garlic, crushed
2 Tbsp (30 ml) olive oil
½ tsp (2 ml) fresh ginger root, minced
Pinch of sea salt
Freshly grated nutmeg (optional)

Remove the coarse stems of the greens (fold them in half and cut out the "spine"). Roll the leaves and chop them into ½ inch thick slices. Steam the greens in a steamer over a pot of boiling water for 5-10 minutes. Drain well.

In a large fry pan, heat the oil, add the garlic and ginger and sauté briefly. Add the mushrooms and sauté for 5-10 minutes until they have released their moisture. Add the greens, mix well and cook for another 8-10 minutes. Season to taste with salt, sprinkle with nutmeg and serve.

Serves 8

Lentil And Rice Pilaf With Toasted Cumin Seeds

Signy: Here is a rice pilaf recipe a friend sent to me. Lentils are the fastest cooking dried legume and for that reason can be cooked with rice into an interesting pilaf. The value for me is getting some protein in the rice, so it can sort of stand alone, or be a side dish to something else. It is adapted from the Joy of Cooking.

2 Tbsp (30 ml) olive oil
1 clove garlic, finely chopped
½ tsp (2 ml) cumin seeds
4 cups (1 L) water
1 cup (250 ml) lentils
1 cup (250 ml) brown basmati rice
2 cups (500 ml) vegetable stock
¼ cup (60 ml) walnuts, lightly toasted
Sea salt to taste

Bring 4 cups of water to the boil. Add the lentils and boil, uncovered, for 10 minutes. Drain and set aside. Heat the olive oil in large saucepan or deep skillet over low heat. Add the garlic and cumin seeds and cook for 1 minute. Add the lentils along with the rice. Stir and add the 2 cups of vegetable stock. Bring to a boil. Stir once, cover, and cook over med-low heat until the stock is absorbed and the rice and lentils are tender, about 15-30 minutes. Uncover and let stand for 5 min. Meanwhile, toast the walnuts in a small skillet over medium heat and stir into the pilaf. Serve with vegetables or as a side dish.

Serves 4

Spicy Peanut Tempeh

Signy: I tried this recipe because I don't like tempeh plain, but I know it's so good for me. I love the sauce in this recipe. It makes it great.

2 pkgs. of tempeh, frozen or fresh (225g each)
2 cups (500 ml) water
3 Tbsp (45 ml) olive oil
1 large onion (approx 1 cup or 250 ml), sliced
1 leek, washed and sliced diagonally, green parts included
4 stalks celery, sliced diagonally
1 cup (250 ml) carrot, sliced diagonally
2 burdock roots, sliced diagonally (optional)

Boil tempeh in water for 10 minutes. Drain. When cool enough to handle, cut into 1 inch squares. Set aside.

In a pot, heat oil on medium heat. Add onions, leeks, celery, carrot and burdock and cook for 5 minutes, stirring frequently to prevent burning. Add cubed tempeh and cook for 5 minutes longer. Serve on grain with Peanut Sauce (see below).

Peanut Sauce

2-4 large cloves garlic
½ cup (125 ml) fresh lemon or lime juice
½ cup (125 ml) umeboshi vinegar (optional)
1 cup (250 ml) smooth natural peanut butter
3 Tbsp (45 ml) flax seeds
1 cup (250 ml) water
2 tsp (10 ml) ginger root
¼ tsp (1 ml) cayenne or 1 hot pepper (optional)
1 cup (250 ml) fresh cilantro leaves

In a blender or food processor, grind garlic. Add the lime juice, umeboshi vinegar, peanut butter, flax seeds, water, ginger and cayenne. Process until smooth.
Pour sauce over tempeh mixture and stir until hot. Add the fresh cilantro leaves, adjust seasonings, and serve over noodles or rice.

Serves 8

Super Snacks and Spreads

General healthy substitutions for baking

Try using these substitutions to transform your family favourites into cancer-conquering treats.

- Use soy, rice, almond or oat milk instead of dairy milk.

- To increase flax seed consumption and reduce eggs use:

    1 Tbsp ground flax seed plus 3 Tbsp water = 1 egg (and trust me, it binds just as well). Double this combination if 2 eggs are required.

- Try spelt flour or whole wheat pastry flour (made from a different wheat variety) instead of unbleached white flour.

- Experiment with applesauce, brown rice syrup, stevia, honey and maple syrup as sweeteners or a puree of dates or raisins mixed with a fruit juice.

Cranberry Cornmeal Muffins

Dennis: These muffins make for a perfect snack and the raisins help along a sweet tooth. They are easy to make and freeze well. I highly recommend taking the time to look for the whole wheat pastry flour.

1¾ cups (435 ml) whole wheat pastry flour
¾ cup (185 ml) cornmeal
2 tsp (10 ml) baking powder
¼ tsp (1 ml) sea salt
1 ½ cups (375 ml) fresh or frozen cranberries
½ cup (125 ml) honey
1 Tbsp (15 ml) grated lemon or lemon zest
2 Tbsp (30 ml) ground flax seed mixed with 6 Tbsp (90 ml) water
1¼ cups (310 ml) rice milk
1¼ cup (60 ml) olive oil or other unrefined oil
⅓ cup (80 ml) golden raisins

Preheat oven to 400 F (200 C). Grease muffin tin.

In a large bowl, combine dry ingredients and cranberries. In a separate bowl, whisk together flax mixture, rice milk, honey, lemon zest and oil. Pour over dry ingredients and stir together until just moistened. Fold in raisins. Spoon into muffin cups and bake for 20 minutes, or until golden and firm to the touch. Turn out to cool on cake rack.

Makes 12 muffins

Signy's Home-Made Power Bars

Signy: It is great to have the healthy snacks handy and it means I don't have to resort to "power (read sugar) bars" when my blood sugar levels drop. There are so few good snacks or quick food that you can buy when you are away from home, so I love having my own on hand.

Dry Ingredients
3 cups (750 ml) quick cooking oatmeal
1 cup (250 ml) finely chopped dried apricots or any dried fruit
2 Tbsp (30 ml) sesame seeds
4 Tbsp (60 ml) sunflower seeds
4 Tbsp (60 ml) pumpkin seeds
2 Tbsp (30 ml) almond slivers
2 Tbsp (30 ml) ground flax seeds
4 Tbsp (60 ml) coconut
1 tsp (5 ml) cinnamon

Wet Ingredients
½ cup (125 ml) organic butter over low heat (Preferred: cold-pressed walnut oil)
¾ cup (185 ml) maple syrup
¾ tsp (3 ml) salt
1 tsp (5 ml) lemon zest
1½ Tbsp (22 ml) organic molasses
2 tsp (10 ml) vanilla

Heat oven to 350 F (180 C). In a large bowl, combine all of the dry ingredients and then set aside.

In a large heavy saucepan, heat the oil or butter and stir in the wet ingredients and bring to a boil over medium heat, stirring frequently. Remove from heat and stir in the dry oat mixture. Mix well. Turn into a 13x9-inch baking pan; press mixture to form an even layer. Bake for 20 minutes. Cut into bars while still warm. Then allow to cool. Keep refrigerated.

Serves 12

Kicks-Ass, Anti-Breast Cancer Muffins

Signy: My friend Zoe, also a cancer survivor, gave this to me. What makes this recipe so great to prevent and treat breast cancer is the ton of ground flax seed you find in it. Also, naturally, it does not have oil, butter or sugar in it. Hello!!!! What a great recipe! I like to try to eat one a day, to keep the monsters away!

1¼ cups (310 ml) water
½ cup (125 ml) unsulphured apricots, chopped
3 cups (750 ml) ground flax
1 cup (250 ml) whole wheat flour
1 tsp (5 ml) baking powder
1 tsp (5 ml) baking soda
½ tsp (2 ml) salt
2 eggs (optional)
⅓ to ½ cup (80-125 ml) organic molasses
½ can (200 ml) pumpkin puree
1 very ripe banana
1 tsp (5 ml) cinnamon
½ tsp (2 ml) ground ginger
½ tsp (2 ml) ground allspice

Heat oven to 350 F (180 C). Bring water to the boil and pour water over apricots. Set aside to cool.

In a large bowl, mix together ground flax seeds, flour, baking powder, baking soda and salt. In a separate bowl mix the molasses and pumpkin puree and mash in the banana. Add cinnamon, ginger and allspice.

Make a well in the dry mixture and pour in the cooled apricot mixture and the puree mixture. Spoon into a greased muffin tin. Bake in oven for 20 minutes.

It can be quite a moist recipe, and so play with the ingredients until you find the right combo for you. Kamut, spelt or rye flours also work and try less molasses and adding some maple syrup.

Makes 12 muffins

Toasted Pita Shapes

These pita triangles are the perfect substitute for high fat potato and corn chips. The monosaturated fats in the olive oil help protect against heart disease and the whole wheat pitas add fibre and B vitamins. A great snack with hummus or salsa any time of the day.

1 package whole wheat pita breads
¼ cup (60 ml) olive oil
¼ tsp (2 ml) salt
¼ tsp (2 ml) Italian herbs

Cut the pita breads into triangles, or use a cookie cutter for different shapes. Mix the oil with the salt and seasonings and lightly brush the pita shapes with the mix. Broil for 3-5 minutes until golden brown.

Serves 8-10

Hummus

I refer to hummus as "food of the Gods." It's packed with good protein from the chickpeas and tahini, plenty of minerals and calcium. The lemon juice also adds antioxidants and vitamin C, and the olive oil has heart health and cancer-preventative effects. If you want a lower fat version, exchange more water for oil.

2-3 cups (500-750 ml) cooked chickpeas (garbanzo beans)
juice 2-3 lemons
3 cloves garlic
1 tsp (5 ml) salt
2-3 Tbsp (30-45 ml) tahini
1 cup (250 ml) oil/water

Place first 5 ingredients in a blender. Add oil/water until smooth. Taste and add extra seasoning. For pink hummus add ¼ cup of steamed beets.

Serve heaped in a bowl and decorate with parsley. Serve with chopped vegetable sticks and toasted pita shapes, see page 144. Also use as a protein and mineral-rich sandwich spread. Can stay refrigerated up to 1 week.

Serves 10

Pat's Calcium Smoothie page 166

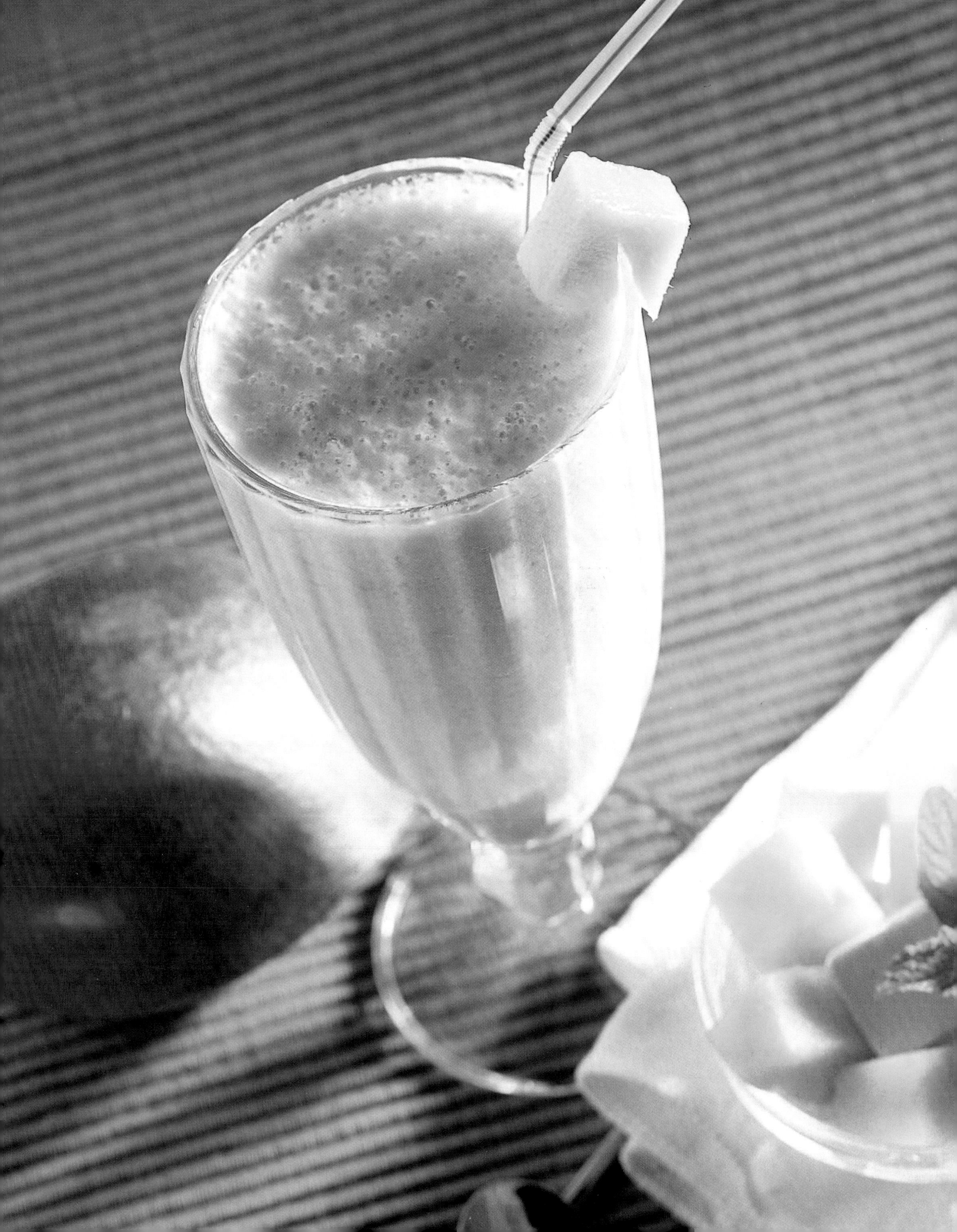

Hummus with Toasted Pita Shapes page 144

Peach and Raspberry Cobbler page 154

Cure-All Oatmeal page 156

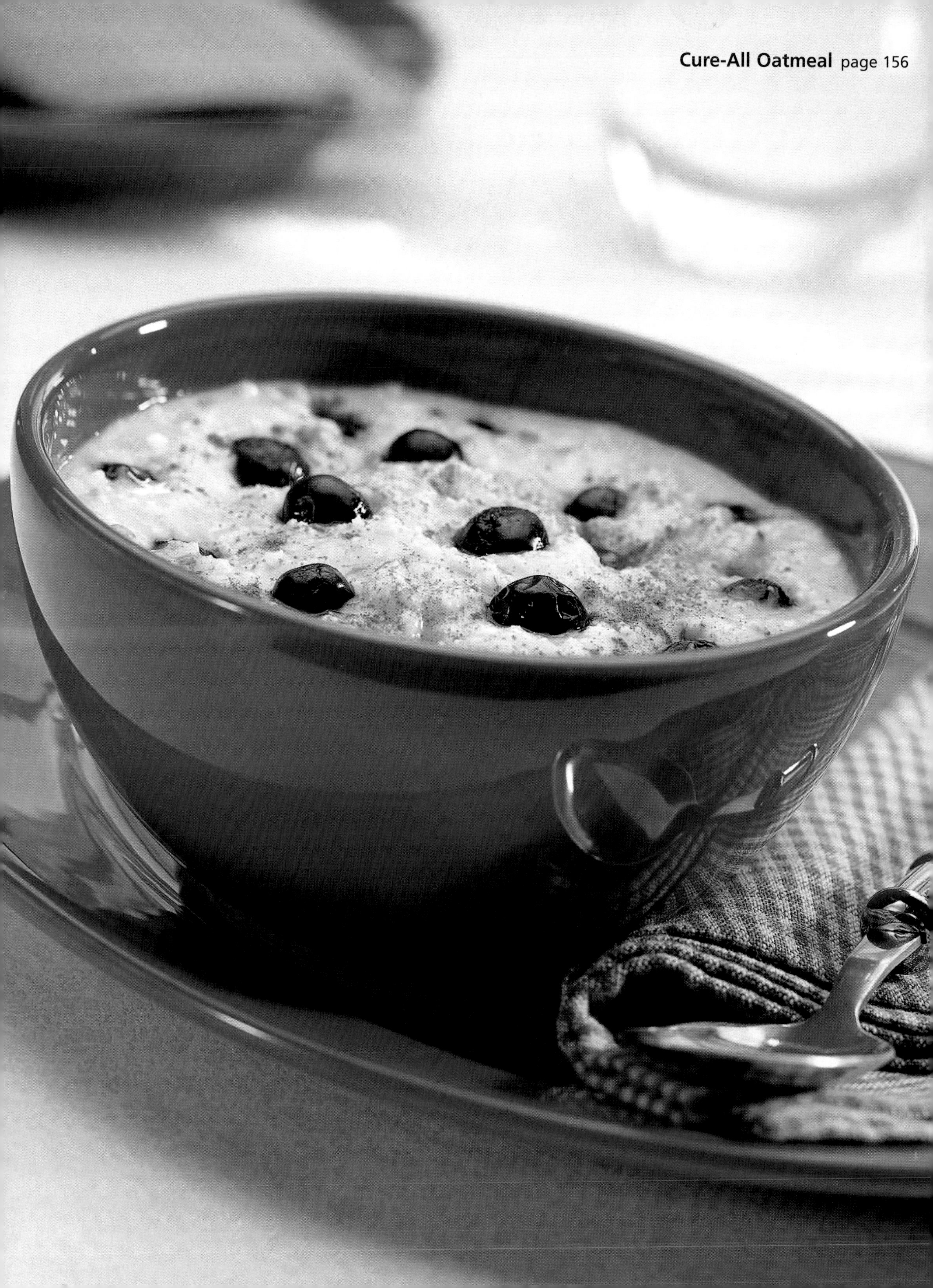

Roasted Beans and Peas

This is an incredibly nutritious snack that is high in protein, fibre and minerals and low in saturated fats. You will need to experiment with the amount of spices you use. Some like it hot...others don't. The combination here is very mild, but I only add the spices to the beans a half teaspoon at a time.

6 cups (1500 ml) cooked, whole beans (soy or chickpeas or green peas - not split peas)
3 Tbsp (30 ml) olive oil
1 Tsp (5 ml) salt
1 Tsp (5ml) curry
¼ Tsp (1 ml) cumin
¼ Tsp (1 ml) cinnamon or garam marsala

Coat a cookie sheet with the olive oil, then toss the beans in the olive oil until well-coated.

Slow-roast the beans in a 200 F (100 C) oven for 4-8 hours. Remove from the oven when crunchy all the way through. Toss in salt and spices. Add the spice mix ½ a teaspoon at a time until you get the desired taste.

Store in an airtight container in your fridge for up to 14 days.

Serves: 3-4 cups

Baked Oven Fries

Home-made fries have never been so delicious. The humble potato is high in zinc and vitamin C, making it an ideal immune booster. For extra flavour and nutrition power, use sweet potatoes in the mix too. Their high beta-carotene content protects against disease. Using sesame seeds adds a little protein and calcium.

6-10 organic russet potatoes
2-4 Tbsp (30-60 ml) olive oil
1-2 tsp (5-10 ml) sea salt
1-2 Tbsp (15-30 ml) sesame seeds

Clean potatoes and cut into wedges. In a bowl drizzle the wedges with oil. Sprinkle with salt and sesame seeds until wedges well coated. Place wedges on a non-stick or oiled baking tray. Bake in 350 F (180 C) oven for 20 minutes. Flip wedges after 10 minutes. Cook for another 10 minutes until golden brown.

Serves 4-8

Air Popped Pop Corn

Using an air popper avoids the hydrogenated and saturated fats found in pre-packaged microwave popcorns. Popcorn is another great high fibre natural snack. Add flax oil (instead of butter) and flavourings such as:

- Sea salt, dulse flakes and tamari soy sauce
- Cinnamon and honey
- Garlic powder and nutritional yeast
- Cajun grilling spices
- Italian herbs and red pepper flakes

Garlic Toast with Fresh Herbs

This recipe is versatile and can replace butter on dinner rolls, sandwiches or toast. The roasted garlic provides creaminess with a mild flavour (and far less odour than raw garlic) and the parsley adds chlorophyll and vitamin C. Experiment with other fresh Italian herbs, such as oregano and basil.

10 roasted garlic cloves (see below)
¼-½ cup (60-125 ml) olive oil
½ cup (125 ml) parsley, finely chopped
v tsp (2 ml) salt (optional)

In a small bowl, mix all the ingredients together. Mash gently with a fork until well combined. Spread on pre-toasted whole-grain bread, bread rolls or mini-pita breads.

Serves 2

Roasted Garlic

To oven roast garlic, Preheat the oven to 300 F (150 C). Peel a whole bulb of garlic, separate the cloves and peel them. Toss the cloves in a small amount of olive oil. Place on a baking tray and cook for 10-15 minutes. The cloves are done when they are soft and lightly brown. These can then be mashed together and used as a garlic "butter" or added to favourite recipes for an immune boost and to give subtle garlic flavour and add creaminess.

Best Basil Pesto

Pesto can be used with pasta as a quick and tasty sauce, or as a spread on a whole grain toast topped with fresh tomato and ground black pepper as a snack or appetizer. You can also mix this recipe with an equal amount of medium or soft tofu as a dip for crackers.

10 garlic cloves
½ cup (125 ml) onion, coarsely chopped
¾ cup (185 ml) fresh walnuts or sunflower seeds (unroasted)
1-2 cups (250-500 ml) olive oil
2-3 cups (500-750 ml) cups basil leaves
½ cup (125 ml) nutritional yeast (or parmesan cheese)
1-2 tsp (5-10 ml) salt (to taste)

Place garlic, onion, and nuts or seeds into a food processor and blend until fine. Add the basil leaves and nutritional yeast. With the food processor on, add the oil slowly until the sauce is quite thick.

Use immediately or store in a glass jar with a little olive oil poured on top. This prevents oxidization of the basil. Consume within 2-3 days.

Serves 10

Black Bean Dip

This dip is very versatile and can be used as a high protein sandwich spread with fresh peppers, sprouts and lettuce. It's also a great party food. The salsa provides a good source of lycopene (helps prevent prostate cancer) and the lime juice and cilantro provide plenty of vitamin C.

1 14 oz (454 ml) can black beans, drained and rinsed
½ cup (125 ml) sugar-free tomato salsa, hot or mild
2 Tbsp (30 ml) lime juice
2 Tbsp (30 ml) fresh cilantro, chopped
¼ tsp (1 ml) ground cumin
Salt and freshly ground black pepper to taste

In a food processor, combine the black beans, salsa, lime juice, cilantro, and cumin. Process until smooth. Season with salt and pepper and transfer to small bowl. Garnish with cilantro, green onions or red peppers. (The dip can be stored, covered, in the refrigerator for up to 2 days.)

Makes about 1 and ½ cups

Mini Cornmeal Muffins

These little muffins are perfect with soups and salads and provide a change from wheat based breads.

5 Tbsp (75 ml) olive oil
1 medium red bell pepper, seeded and finely chopped
1 fresh hot chile pepper, seeded and minced, or 2
½ tsp (2 ml) dry red chile peppers
1 cup (250 ml) soy milk
2 Tbsp (30 ml) freshly squeezed lemon juice

1 cup (250 ml) whole wheat pastry flour
1 cup (250 ml) yellow coarsely ground cornmeal
1 tsp (5 ml) baking powder
1 tsp (5 ml) baking soda
1 tsp (5 ml) salt
1 ear corn, kernels cut off the cob, or ¾ cup (185 ml) frozen (thawed)
   or canned corn

Preheat oven to 350 F (180 C). Lightly oil mini-muffin tins with oil and dust with cornmeal, shaking out the excess. Put the soy milk, remaining olive oil, and the lemon juice into a small bowl and stir together. It should thicken slightly.

Whisk the flour, cornmeal, baking powder, baking soda, and salt together in a large bowl until combined. Add the soy milk mixture and combine just until mixed. You don't want to over mix the batter. Fold in the peppers and canned corn. Spread the batter evenly in the prepared tins. Bake the bread about 20 to 25 minutes. Test with a toothpick or sharp knife in the middle to see that it comes out clean. Cool and serve.

Makes 12 muffins

Dreamy Desserts

Baked Pears

Pat: This simple dessert is delicious with natural plain yogurt and sliced almonds.

2 pears
2-4 cups (500ml-1L) grape juice or sweet red wine

Peel two large pears. Cut in half longwise and take out core. Place upside down in shallow baking dish. Pour medium sweet red wine, or grape juice over top until half covered.

Bake uncovered at 325 F (170 C). It is ready when pears are soft and the wine or the juice has almost evaporated.

Serves 4

Stewed fruits

Marie: This recipe is great for fruit that has been around a few days! I make a batch and then warm portions as required. For an awesome breakfast, add a slice of flax bread with organic strawberry jam and don't forget the all important pot of green tea!

1-2 apples
1-2 pears
¼ to 1 cup (60-250 ml) dried fruits such as prunes, raisins or cranberries

Peel, core and slice apples or pears, but not too thinly. Place the cut fruits with the dried fruit in a pot. Add enough water to cover, and simmer until the apples and pears are just tender. Add a dash of cinnamon and honey to taste.

Serves 2-4

Raspberry and Apple Crisp

Mel: I grew up on apple crisp. During my convalescence this apple raspberry crisp hit the spot both taste-wise and emotionally.

Filling:
6 cups (1.5 L) apples, peeled and sliced
300 g raspberries, unsweetened frozen (or 1½ cups (375 g) fresh raspberries)
⅓ cup (85 ml) sugar or honey
2 Tbsp (30 ml) whole wheat or spelt flour
2 tsp (10 ml) cinnamon

Crumble:
1 cup (250 ml) quick cooking oats
¼ cup (60 ml) brown sugar or brown rice syrup
1 tsp (5 ml) cinnamon
¼ cup (60 ml) soft margarine or cold-pressed walnut or safflower oil

Pre-heat oven to 350 F (180 C). Place the fruit in a large mixing bowl. In a separate bowl mix the sweetener, flour and cinnamon. Add to the fruit and mix in well. Place the fruit mixture in a large baking dish.

Using the same large bowl, mix together the crumble ingredients (oats, sweetener, cinnamon and oil) using you fingers or two knives to mix thoroughly. Sprinkle over the fruit mixture.

Bake in the oven for 50-60 minutes. Serve warm or cold.

Serves 6

Sensational Fruit Pudding

Mel: Before the cancer I had a very sweet tooth. After my throat and stomach surgery I could no longer tolerate or enjoy sugary sweet things. Fruit however, continued to delight my new "plumbing," and this recipe was a staple for me throughout my chemotherapy.

1 cup (250 ml) soft or medium firm tofu
¼ cup (60 ml) sweetener, or reduce to taste
pinch of (1 ml) salt
¾ cup (185 ml) mangoes and/or strawberries
½ tsp (2 ml) natural vanilla extract
½ tsp (2 ml) lemon juice

In a blender or food processor, add all the ingredients and blend well. When creamy, pour into serving dish. Refrigerate until firm (at least one hour).

Serves 4

Rice Pudding with Raisins and Walnuts

Dennis: This makes enough rice pudding for a week, and I eat it twice a day with rice milk, apple sauce, banana, and blueberries. It's great for a snack or dessert, and it's easy to make. Keep it covered in the refrigerator.

2-3 cups (500-750 ml) cooked grains, such as brown rice
1 cup (250 ml) walnuts, chopped
1 cup (250 ml) raisins
1½ cups (375 ml) rice milk
1 tsp (5 ml) cinnamon
1 Tbsp (15 ml) vanilla

Follow recipe for Perfectly Fluffy Grains (page 115). Return grains to a saucepan. Add all of the above ingredients to the rice, and cook on low heat for 15 minutes, stirring frequently to prevent sticking. Remove from heat. Serve warm or cool. Cover and refrigerate.

Serves 6

Cranberry Apple Bread

Dennis: This recipe is easy to make and always comes out perfect. This is a great party dish, and everyone wants the recipe.

2 cups (500 ml) peeled, chopped apples
½ cup (125 ml) honey
¼ cup (60 ml) unsweetened apple sauce
2 Tbsp (30 ml) olive oil
1 egg, or 1 Tbsp ground flax mixed with 3 Tbsp water
1½ cups (375 ml) whole wheat pastry flour
1½ tsp (7 ml) baking powder
½ tsp (2 ml) baking soda
1 tsp (5 ml) cinnamon
1 cup (250 ml) fresh or frozen cranberries
½ cup (125 ml) chopped walnuts

Preheat oven to 350 F (180 C). Combine apples, sweeteners and oil in a medium sized mixing bowl. Add egg or flax mix, mixing well. Combine dry ingredients in a separate bowl. Add to apple mixture, stirring just until the ingredients are moistened. Stir in cranberries and walnuts.

Spread batter evenly into a lightly oiled and lightly floured loaf pan. Bake for 1 hour or until a tooth pick or a sharp knife inserted into the centre of the bread comes out clean.

Serves 8

Carrot Cake

Dennis: This is the best carrot cake I have ever tasted, and my friends say the same thing. It is a beautiful moist cake that doesn't need any frosting.

Wet ingredients
½ cup (125 ml) apple sauce
½ cup (125 ml) honey
½ cup (125 ml) olive oil or other unrefined oil
2 eggs, or 2 Tbsp ground flax seed with 6 Tbsp water
¼ tsp (1 ml) sea salt
1 tsp (5 ml) cinnamon

Dry ingredients
1 cup (250 ml) whole wheat pastry flour
1 cup (250 ml) raw carrot, grated
1 tsp (5 ml) baking powder
¾ tsp (3 ml) baking soda
¼ cup (60 ml) walnuts, chopped
1 cup (250 ml) crushed pineapple, drained

In a bowl, mix together the dry ingredients. In a separate large bowl, mix the wet ingredients well. Add the dry ingredients to the wet. Mix together.

Bake at 350 F (180 C). in a greased square pan, eight-by-eight inch (20 x 20 cm) until a toothpick or sharp knife inserted in centre comes out clean. Approximately 40 minutes. Cool and serve.

Serves 8

Fruit Salad with Cherries

Cherries are a rich source of the flavanoids anthocyanidins and proanthocyanidins that give this fruit their deep purple colour. These pigments protect against skin deterioration, thus slowing down the aging process. Try and make a fruit salad as colourful as possible for maximum protective and nutritional benefit.

Equal amounts of pineapple, canteloupe, grapes, cherries, orange, bananas and honey dew melon (or kiwi fruit) cut into bite size pieces.

Mix together in a large salad bowl. Add a squeeze or two of lemon juice to help prevent browning. This also enhances the sweetness of the fruit. Refrigerate and serve cool. Serve in elegant glasses or bowls.

Serves 4-6

Cranberry Bars

These yummy little bars pack a whole host of vitamin C , minerals and plenty of fibre. The coconut butter is a more natural form of the traditional lard or shortening and adds to richness of the bar. Coconut butter is available from most health food stores. Use in moderation.

Cranberry Filling
3 cups (750 ml) frozen cranberries
¼ cup (60 ml) raisins
¼ cup (60 ml) dried apricots, chopped
¼ cup (60 ml) crystallized ginger, chopped
½ cup (125 ml) sucanat or honey
1 cup (250 ml) apple juice

Base and Topping
2 cups (500 ml) whole wheat or spelt flour
¼ cup (125 ml) sucanat or brown rice syrup
1½ tsp (7ml) ground ginger
¼ tsp (1 ml) salt
¾ cup (185 ml) coconut butter
1 cup (250 ml) rolled oats
¾ cup (185 ml) raw sunflower seeds

Heat oven to 350 F (180 C). For the filing, combine cranberries, dried fruits, honey and apple juice in a medium saucepan. Bring to the boil over medium heat. Stir until the mixture thickens and the cranberries pop, about 5 to 10 minutes.

In a large bowl mix together all of the base ingredients, blending in the coconut butter with the tips of your fingers. The mix should look like moist crumbs. Set aside 1 and ½ cups of this mix for the topping. Grease a 9"x13" baking pan, and press the crumb mixture into the base. Bake at 350 F (180 C) for 15 minutes.

Remove the base from the oven, spread the cranberry mix over it and cover with the remaining 1 and ½ cups of topping mixture.

Bake for another 30 minutes. Allow to cool before serving.

Makes 12 bars

Peach and Raspberry Cobbler

Dennis:This is a delicious way to eat peaches. This recipe turns out perfect every time, and takes little time to prepare.

¼ cup (60 ml) honey
2 Tbsp (30 ml) arrowroot powder
1 cup (250 ml) hot water
3 cups (750 ml) sliced peaches
2 cups (500 ml) raspberries
½ tsp (2 ml) cinnamon

1¼ cups (310 ml) whole wheat pastry flour
1 Tbsp (15 ml) honey
1½ tsp (7 ml) baking powder
¼ tsp (1 ml) salt
2 Tbsp (30 ml) cold-pressed canola oil
½ cup (125 ml) soy or rice milk

Preheat oven to 400 F (200 C). Mix the arrowroot powder in the hot water and add to a saucepan on medium heat. Stir in the sweetener and fruits.

Bring to a boil, stirring continuously, until the mixture thickens. Add cinnamon and pour into a baking dish.

Mix the flour, salt, and baking powder in a large bowl. Add the 2 tablespoons of oil and mix in with the flour, crumbling the mix between your fingers, until it is fine and crumbly.

Mix the honey with the soy or rice milk. Stir the rice or soy milk into the flour and gently pour it over the fruits. Spread it if necessary, but it does not have to perfectly cover the fruits.

Bake about 25 minutes, until golden brown.

Breakfasts of Champions

Stainmaster Breakfast

*Robert: The idea behind this breakfast goes beyond just nutrition.
Yes, nutrition and "staying power" throughout the day are critically
important, but in addition to that the ingredients are carefully chosen
to target lymphoma cells (possibly other cancers as well), according
to evidence-based scientific research.*

¾ cup (185 ml) organic brown rice
¼ cup (60 ml) wild rice
2 Tbsp (30 ml) turmeric powder
1 tsp (5 ml) sea salt
blueberries, raspberries, blackberries, strawberries, cranberries

Thaw any frozen berries the night before. Bring 4 cups of water to the boil. Add salt and turmeric powder. Add the brown and wild rice and cover. Turn down to low and cook for 45 minutes. Cool and store in the fridge in a GLASS container. The penetrating power of turmeric is so strong that it will permanently discolor plastic and may cause the leaching of very toxic organochlorines from the plastic.

For breakfast, serve some rice, add the fruit (and another teaspoon or two of turmeric if you like) and either soymilk or rice milk. Mix 'er up and enjoy.

Savoury Version
Cut several slices of shiitake mushroom into the day's portion of rice in the morning, and heat. (preferably not in the microwave.) Cover the rice with a generous sprinkling of turmeric and fresh ground black pepper. Other spices can be added (oregano, cayenne etc.) as desired.

Serves 6

Walnut French Toast

Dennis: This is a gourmet treat that you will want to make often.

⅓ cup (80 ml) rice milk
1 egg or 1 Tbsp (15 ml) flax seed in 3 Tbsp (45 ml) water
1 tsp (5 ml) honey
¼ cup (60 ml) whole wheat pastry flour
⅛ tsp (1 ml) sea salt
1½ cups (375 ml) walnuts, finely chopped or ground
Olive oil
4 slices of whole grain bread

Combine the rice milk, flax, honey, flour and salt in a blender for 10 seconds. Transfer this batter to a shallow bowl. Place chopped walnuts in another shallow bowl. Quickly place bread in batter and coat both sides, then coat with walnuts on both sides. In a hot skillet, sauté the bread on both sides in the oil, until it is golden. Transfer the bread to a warm plate and sprinkle with cinnamon. Serve with applesauce and blueberries, stewed fruits (see page 149) or maple syrup.

Serves 2

Cure-All Oatmeal

This recipe makes four cups of ready-to-cook oatmeal. Buy wheat germ from a health store that keeps it in the fridge. Store flax seeds and wheat germ in freezer.

Dry Ingredients
3-4 cups (185 ml) organic oatmeal (large flake, quick cook or steel cut)
½ cup (125 ml) organic fresh ground flax seed
½ cup (125 ml) fresh raw wheat germ
1 - 2 Tbsp(15-30 ml) cinnamon
¼ cup (60 ml) Red Star nutritional yeast (optional - do not use if you
  have yeast/fungal problems)

Water, rice, soy or almond milk

Mix all the dry ingredients in an air-tight container. Shake to mix well.

In a bowl combine ⅓ cup of the oatmeal mix and ⅔ cup of water, rice, soy, or almond milk . Heat in microwave 1½ to 2 minutes or cook on the stove top, stirring regularly over medium heat, for 5-8 minutes.

To add calories and nutrients - add raisins, banana, tahini, or toasted seeds and nuts.

Serves 10

Nutty Granola

This granola is low in added fat as it is roasted in juice rather than oil. The coconut and nuts provide a good mix of healthy polyunsaturated and essential fats that help boost the immune system and lower blood pressure. The grain flakes provide sustained energy and help regulate blood sugar.

5 cups (1250 ml) mixed rolled or flaked grains (eg. oats, barley, kamut, rye, spelt)
2 cups (500 ml) coconut flakes (optional)
2 cups (500 ml) nuts, chopped
¼ cup (60 ml) blackstrap molasses
½ cup (125 ml) apple, pear or orange juice

Preheat oven to 250 F or 130 C. Mix the dry ingredients in a bowl and blend the wet ingredients in a separate bowl. Spread the mixture out evenly on two large non-stick baking sheets. Bake for about an hour, stirring and turning the granola every 15 minutes or so. DON'T let it burn! Keeps well in the refrigerator or a cool dry place for 7 to 10 days.

Serve with fresh fruit, stewed fruits (see page 149), apple or grape juice, or soy, rice or dairy milk.

Serves 12

Berry Puree

1¼ cups fresh or frozen berries
apple juice

Use one and a quarter cups of fresh summer berries (or defrosted summer berries), these can be strawberries, raspberries, blueberries or black berries. Blend the berries in a blender. Sweeten with a little apple juice if necessary. Other great pancake and waffle toppings include almond nut butter, chopped walnut pieces and bananas.

Serves 4

Good Grains Pancake or Waffle Mix

This recipe provides the convenience of ready-made pancake mix, but in a much more nutritious form. Of course you may want to double the mix so that you have more on hand in the future. Using a variety of grains (such as spelt instead of wheat flour) adds more nutrients and a better protein profile.

2½ cups (750ml) spelt flour
1 cup (250 ml) whole wheat flour
½ cup (125 ml) flax seed, finely ground
½ cup (125 ml) yellow cornmeal
2 Tbsp (60 ml) sucanat (optional)
2 Tbsp (60 ml) baking powder
1 tsp (5 ml) baking soda
3 tsp (15 ml) salt

In large bowl, stir together all ingredients. Divide into thirds (about 1 and ⅔ cups each) and seal in zipper-lock bags. Store in refrigerator or freezer.

Serves 12

Good Grains Pancakes or Waffles

1¼ cups (310 ml) soy or rice milk
¼ cup (60 ml) liquid egg substitute or 2 eggs
2 Tbsp (60 ml) vegetable oil
1 batch (about 1⅔ cups) Good Grains Pancake or Waffle Mix

In large bowl, whisk together milk, egg substitute and oil. Whisk in Good Grains mix until dry ingredients are just moistened. Batter should be slightly lumpy; do not overmix.

For pancakes: Use ¼ cup batter per pancake. Cook pancakes on hot griddle until bubbles on top burst. Turn and cook other side until lightly browned.

For waffles: Cook according to manufacturer's directions for your waffle iron.

Serve with applesauce and blueberries, stewed fruits (see page 149) or maple syrup. Try spreading waffles with a thin layer of tahini for some protein and calcium.

Makes 12

Rolling Oatmeal Porridge

Signy: Here is my "get you rolling" in the morning oatmeal porridge. I have been making it for years, it is the only way I can make porridge that I like, full of yummy things. It is definitely elaborate. It is easy to make and has all sorts of good "kick cancer's ass" ingredients.

1 cup (250 ml) water
3 dried unsulphered apricots, chopped up to small pieces
Handful of almonds, chopped
Half a banana, sliced
¼ cup (60 ml) shredded coconut
½ cup (125 ml) rolled oats
1 Tbsp (15 ml) ground flax seeds
¼ tsp (1 ml) cinnamon

In a pot combine water, dried fruits, almonds, banana, coconut, oats, flax seeds and cinnamon. Bring to the boil. Stir and reduce heat so that it is just simmering. Leave it to simmer just under 5 minutes, stirring often. Then take off heat and let sit another just under 5 minutes. Then add maple syrup or sweetener to desired sweetness, stir it around. And finally add soy or rice milk as desired.

Serves 1

Breakfast Herb Scramble

Signy: Now every tofu cook book has its own version of this. Adjust it any way it works for you. When I serve it, I sometimes sprinkle chopped up fresh parsley, or a handful of sunflower seeds or chopped up almonds on top.

2 Tbsp (30 ml) sesame oil
2-3 green onions, diced
½ cup (125 ml) green pepper finely chopped
7-9 mushrooms, chopped
400-450 grams medium firm tofu, mashed with fork
2-3 Tbsp (30-45 ml) tamari soy sauce

½ tsp (2 ml) sea salt
½ tsp (2 ml) curry powder
several dashes cayenne pepper
several dashes turmeric (for colour)

Heat oil and tamari soy sauce and saute onions, pepper and mushroom in frying pan for about 3 minutes.

In a separate bowl, mash the tofu and add the curry powder, turmeric, salt and cayenne. Stir well until the tofu becomes a light yellow colour. Add the tofu mix to the pan with the vegetables. Saute for 3-6 minutes more, until the flavors mingle and the mixture is hot throughout.

Serve immediately with baked corn chips, thick toast, pita triangles, veggie sticks, salad or tomato slices.

Serves 2-3

Flaxen French Toast

Once you've made this recipe the first time you'll be addicted to healthy French toast. Using the flax instead of the eggs provides cancer-fighting fibre and plenty of powerful phtyo-chemicals. The grains in the bread and the nutritional yeast provide minerals and the B vitamins, important for stress and the nervous system.

Flax Mix
½ cup (125 ml) finely ground flax meal
¾ cup (185 ml) water
Blend together until the mix looks like a thick milkshake

¼ to ½ cup (60 - 125 ml) soymilk
1 tsp (5 ml) cinnamon
2 Tbsp (30 ml) maple syrup
2 Tbsp (30 ml) nutritional yeast
2 Tbsp (30 ml) oat flour
Thickly sliced whole grain bread

Combine oat flour, nutritional yeast and a little soymilk to make a paste. Add the flax mix, cinnamon , maple syrup and soymilk. Using a whisk, mix the ingredients into a batter. It should have a flexible, egg-like consistency. Try not to add too much soymilk. Heat a lightly-oiled cast iron skillet (or non-stick frying pan). Dip the bread in the batter and place on the hot skillet. Cook each side until brown. Check after two to three minutes. Add more oil if needed. Sprinkle with cinnamon and serve with warm maple syrup and fresh fruit.

Serves 4

Berry Breakfast Wrap

Using natural nut butter, such as almond butter is recommended for this recipe. Almond butter adds protein, good fats and calcium. Soy yogurt is also now readily available in most supermarkets and is a good way to get the benefits of soy in a convenient way.

1 cup (250 ml) granola
1 cup (250 ml) soy yoghurt (any flavour)
2 Tbsp (60 ml) almond butter
1 banana
1 tsp (5 ml) honey or maple syrup
½-1 cup (125-250 ml) fresh berries
2 x 10 inch whole wheat tortillas or wraps

In a large bowl, combine the yogurt, granola, maple syrup and banana. Fold in the berries. Divide the nut butter between the tortillas and spread evenly over each. Leave a 1 inch border around the edge.

Divide the granola mixture between the tortillas. Place mixture on the lower half of the wrap. Wrap from the bottom, tucking in the outer right and left edges in as you roll. Wrap in some foil or wax paper for a wrap to go.

Serves 2

Bold Beverages

Sally's Superfood Smoothie

Choose a green powder that is made from organic whole foods and features high chlorophyll foods such as wheatgrass, spirulina and barley greens. Avoid too many herbal additions as these may contraindicate medications. I like a stevia sweetened greens powder that doesn't change the flavour or look of the smoothie. See page 177 for recommendations.

1 cup (250 ml) soy, rice, grain or almond milk
⅓ cup (160 ml) frozen blueberries
1 small fresh or frozen banana (frozen banana makes the smoothie creamy)
2 tsp (10 ml) Greens Powder
1-2 Tbsp (15-30 ml) ground flax seed
½ tsp (2 ml) tahini (optional-for calcium)
½-1 cup (125-250 ml) filtered water
Sweetener to taste

Blend all the ingredients together in a blender, food processor or use a hand-immersion bender. Drink and enjoy

Serves 1

Brad's Daily Booster Smoothie

Brad: I did some research on a supplement that seems to be a derivative of brown rice and maitake mushrooms. Apparently it boosts the natural killer cell activity by around 20 percent. The supplement is expensive, so I made my own version and it worked! I drink this smoothie and then take my vitamins and Maitake Mushroom Extract (200 mg). I have had an increase in my white cells so that they are almost back within a normal range....something my hematologist said would not happen after chemo!

1 banana
¼ cup (60 ml) frozen organic blueberries
3 Tbsp (45 ml) ground flax seed
1 Tbsp (15 ml) brown rice polish*
½ cup (125 ml) - 1 cup (250 ml) enriched soy milk
1 tsp (5 ml) of vitamin C powder**
1 Tbsp (15 ml) Greens Powder

Combine all ingredients in a blender. Blend till smooth and enjoy!!

Serves 1

*This is found in health food stores and is the flour made from the membrane removed from brown rice to make it white rice.
** This is the straight powder with no sugar or colourings added. Work up to this amount as it can cause the diarrhea. You may even want to check your total vitamin C intake with your health care professional first.

Flaxy Mary

Marie: I love to enjoy this one in my favourite "elegant" glass. It helps me unwind at the end of the day.

2 Tbsp (30 ml) ground flax seed
1½ cups (385 ml) tomato juice
Squeeze of lemon

Stir in the ground flax seeds into a glass of tomato juice, add a squeeze of fresh lemon or lime juice and enjoy!

Serves 1

Crantini

Marie: This is another elegant evening favourite of mine.

Natural mineral water such as Perrier
Cranberry Juice
Frozen Cranberries

Mix equal parts organic cranberry juice and Perrier with a few frozen cranberries instead of ice.

Serves 1

Exotic Fruit Spritzer

Spritzers are a natural pop that every one in the family can enjoy. Look for good quality organic juices such as apple and pear juice in season or other more exotic fruit flavours are now available. Spritzers allow you to enjoy maximum flavour without the sugar, caffeine, colouring and preservatives in pop.

1 carton guava, passion fruit or mango juice
1 bottle good quality natural mineral water

In a tall, elegant pitcher, mix half fruit juice and half mineral water. Add ice cubes, fruit for garnish and a swizzle stick. Pour into tall glasses.

Serves 4

Pat's Ginger Tea

Fresh raw ginger, grated
Honey

Grate raw ginger root and add to an equal amount of honey. Store in jar in fridge. When you want to make a cup of tea, just add 2 tablespoons of the honey/ginger mixture to a cup of boiling water. Delicious!

Mel's Ginger Tea

Mel: This was a wonderful anti-nausea drink. It also served as a nice relaxant. As an added bonus, it infused the whole house with a wonderful odour. Many people coming in the door commented on this.

Ginger, sliced or chopped
Honey

Put 4 cups (1 Litre) of water in a large saucepan. Cut 1 chunk (about the length of your thumb) of organic peeled ginger into slices or small pieces. Add to water and boil. Add 1-2 Tbsp. (15-30 ml) honey and simmer for at least 10 minutes. Remove ginger, and serve.

Serves 4

Pat's Hot Apple Cider

Pat: Organic apple cider can be bought at natural foods markets and is readily available in the fall.

Organic apple cider
Cinnamon
Cloves
Nutmeg

Heat a cup of organic apple cider with tiny bit of cinnamon, cloves and nutmeg.

Pat's Calcium Smoothie

1 banana*
2½ cups (625 ml) vanilla soy milk
2 Tbsp (30 ml) sesame seeds
2 Tbsp (30 ml) honey
2 Tbsp (30 ml) unsulphured blackstrap molasses
2 Tbsp (30 ml) soy protein powder

Slice banana and throw into blender. Fill blender to 3 cup level with soy milk. Add sesame seeds, honey, unsulphured blackstrap molasses and soy protein powder. Blend until creamy.

* Variations: replace banana with raspberries or strawberries or ½ small tin of pineapple.

Serves 1-2

Strawberry Body Builder Shake

Mel: This delightful drink served double duties. It built my weight up during chemotherapy and was also used as a weight booster once chemo was over.

1¼ cup (300 g) soft tofu
1½ cups (375 ml) frozen strawberries, thawed including liquid
¾ cup (185 ml) water
1 ripe banana

Place all the ingredients in a blender and blend until smooth.

Serves 4

Signy's Breakfast of Champions Power Shake

Signy: Here is my morning power shake, I had it brought in to me in the hospital after surgery along with freshly juiced carrots. I like the frozen fruit as it cools the shake down and gives it more of a milkshake feel to it; yum! The breakfast of champions!

150 g soft tofu
1 banana
¾ cup (185 ml) fresh or frozen fruit
¾-1 cup (185 -250 ml) of unsweetened soy milk
1 Tbsp (15 ml) flax seed oil
¼ cup (60 ml) organic, non-fat yoghurt OR 2 capsules of acidophilus emptied out into the blender
1 tsp (5 ml) spirulina, blue green algae or greens powder
1 tsp (5 ml) calcium ascorbate (Vitamin C powder)
1 Tbsp (15 ml) hemp protein powder
1½ Tbsp (22 ml) ground flax seeds
Sweetener to taste

Put all ingredients into a blender and blend until smooth! Make a point of cleaning the blender shortly after (don't leave it for clean up later) as the flax oil and seeds bind and leave a hard reside on the blender, so soak well or clean immediately.

Serves 1

Chocolate Smoothie

This recipe is the perfect solution for chocolate cravings anytime. The cocoa is very high in antioxidants and so you can get the benefits and full flavour in this smoothie - without the damaging fats and sugars that come with regular chocolate. Add 1-2 tablespoons of flax oil to strengthen your immune system.

1 frozen banana, chopped into 1 inch pieces
100 grams soft tofu
2-3 cups (500 – 750 ml) soy, rice, almond or oat milk (if using water add a little more banana)
1 Tbsp (15 ml) fresh flax oil
1 Tbsp (15 ml) cocoa powder (add more to taste)
1-2 teaspoons (5 – 10 ml) honey, maple syrup or other sweetener (add to taste)
Sprinkle of fresh nutmeg

Blend first 6 ingredients together in a blender or use a hand blender. Sprinkle with nutmeg and serve.

Serves 2

Super VJ (Vegetable Juice)

Try this juice if you're giving up coffee or de-toxifying from your previous lifestyle habits! It is highly nutritious with plenty of carotenes and powerful plant chemicals that protect against cancer.

1 cup (250 ml) spinach, loosely packed
2 carrots
1 cup (250 ml) parsley, loosly packed
2 tomatoes
½ cucumber
½ red bell pepper
2 sticks of celery

Using a juicer, juice the vegetables in order. For the spinach and parsley, squash them into a ball in your hand and push through the juicer feeder with the carrots and celery.
Serves 2

Chapter Twenty:

Power of the Positive

Power of the Positive

Well done, you've implemented some changes in your diet! However, some of the real power in healing comes through mind and spirit. Let's face it, you can whip yourself into a frenzy trying to do everything right, but if you aren't dealing with stress well, are exhausting yourself with downward spiraling thoughts which limits your ability to relax, then it's time to look outside the "physical" realm for help.

Science has come to realize what the ancient sages have known throughout time- that our body, mind and spirit are intrinsically connected. For true healing to take place, other aspects of the human being, such as attitudes, emotions and joy for life, must be taken into consideration. This is readily apparent from the stories of our cancer survivors.

Attitude is everything

Immune system strength is a critical factor in cancer management and prevention. Is your glass half empty or half full?

Many studies have shown that optimism can have a positive effect on immune system response. A study conducted at the Mayo clinic found that subjects who were categorized as pessimists had a 19 per cent chance of earlier death than those categorized as optimists. Also, optimists have healthier immune systems, are not as adversely affected by stress and suffer half the number of infectious diseases as pessimists!

What is stress?

Stress is something we are exposed to every day; it's part of our awareness and basic survival instinct as an animal. The unfortunate part is, that in our modern society we are exposed to a myriad of stressors, and most of us are experiencing a stress overload and a resulting inability to effectively deal with it.

We think of stress as happening "in our head," we say "I'm going to go crazy!" but in reality stress precipitates a physiological response. Stress is felt in our physical body as well as our mental thoughts. When we perceive a threat (whether that be an attack from a wild animal, boss or mother-in-law) our body initiates the stress response and hormones are released from the adrenal glands. Adrenaline, and its family of corticosteroids, floods the body, setting up a series of physical responses so that the body is ready for "fight or flight." Since neither

a. punching your boss, nor

b. running from the room screaming

is acceptable in our society, our body remains in this heightened state. As a result, breathing is shallow, blood rushes away from digestion and into the muscles, blood vessels constrict, the immune system gets switched off (it's not much help in fighting off a wild animal), pupils dilate and breathing becomes short. Specifically, studies have shown that key elements in the immune response are affected by stress. High levels of corticosteroids inhibit macrophage and lymphocyte activity and cause wasting of the thymus and lymph tissues.

Escapism versus stress management

I used to think that I could manage my stress by going away for the weekend, seeing a great movie or burying my head in a book for hours on end. In reality though, I would return to my stressful situations with no effective tools to deal with the stress, and before I knew it, I felt like running away again. This scenario is better described as escapism, which can be fine on occasion, but it doesn't switch off that physical stress response as effectively as stress management.

Stress management is using a daily practice that brings your mind and body to a state of peace (ie, digestion and immune system are turned on and humming happily). By bringing your body to this point of peace on a daily basis, it gets used to feeling this way and begins to demand it! With this "practice" being familiar to you it can be used when things start to get stressful, such as when you're waiting for test results, or preparing for surgery. Using a simple breath, or some other learned signal, can instantaneously bring your body back to peace and turn that potentially health damaging stress response OFF. Now you have a coping mechanism. Your immune system stays strong, your mind and heart relaxed. Your daily discipline and efforts are beginning to pay big dividends for your health.

Here are some stress management practices that may work for you: meditation, deep breathing exercises, deep prayer, tai chi, journaling and yoga. All are effective; the important thing is to choose something that appeals to you. Recent studies have shown that both meditation and journaling have resulted in increased immune function.

Laughter

Humour researchers (this may well be my next career!) have shown that laughter has regenerative powers, lowers blood pressure, increases sense of well-being, increases natural killer cells and enhances the immune response.

Some cheap therapy might be to rent a funny movie, read the comics strips, find a funny friend, or even laugh at yourself-the best material you can find!

Emotional connection

How can we "get happy?" One of the easiest ways is to connect with others on a regular basis. Social support systems can be critical for determining health outcomes, studies have shown that those who attend support groups have greater longevity than those that don't. Sharing emotionally with others and reducing social isolation has healing results.

Consider obtaining the benefits and positivity of social interaction through volunteering. A recent study from the University of Michigan found that older people who helped others, reduced their risk of dying by more than half when compared to their less giving peers. Consider joining community groups that reflect your interests and hobbies, such as a book or garden club, athletic team or choir.

Being healthy and living longer can be fun!

Affirmations and self-talk

Behavioural psychologists know that negative thoughts and behaviours can be recognized and re-patterned with positive thoughts and actions. People can, in fact, learn optimism. Working with a practitioner to recognize current patterns can be very helpful. Meditation, quieting the mind, and listening in on your thoughts can also be revealing.

One of the easiest ways to insert new thoughts is to use affirmations on a daily basis. These might focus on the health of your immune system, your relationship with spirit, your relationships with others and how you would like to feel in terms of energy and emotion.

Affirmations are only worthwhile if they are used and repeated. Say each one out loud three times - in the morning and before you go to sleep. Say them through the day as you remember (but say them to yourself at this time!).

Affirmations might include

I love myself. I love others.

I am filled with radiant energy.

My immune system functions perfectly.

I am healthy; my body is perfect.

I am filled with Joy.

Visualisation

Maybe you're having difficulty really believing these statements. If that's the case, using visualization can help personalize positive self-talk by adding images. The power of the mind on our health is now being proven scientifically. Visualizations and positive exercises done before surgery increase healing rates and reduce trauma.

Appropriately trained practitioners can help you "re-frame" how you are viewing your treatments and your life, putting a positive spin on events, thus encouraging your body's healing response.

Integrated bodywork embraces many different modalities using touch and energy work to facilitate and support deepening our body-mind awareness and connection. These include massage, Shiatsu, cranio-sacral therapy, reflexology, acupressure, healing touch and others. With the guidance of a healing practitioner

trained in one or more of these modalities, you can begin to connect with your own inner guidance system and move towards wholeness and integration.
Dr. Carl Simonton and his wife have a series of visualizations that have been very helpful for many cancer patients. Their book "Getting Well Again" explains the concepts.

When choosing a practitioner, consider talking to others for a personal referral. If people have had good experiences, they will be happy to talk about them. If a direct referral isn't available look in local health directories, often found at natural food or vitamin stores. Try and meet with a practitioner before you book a session. Ask plenty of questions about their approach and check in with how comfortable you feel with them. Only continue sessions if you are getting benefit. See Recommended Resources for more information on the body mind spirit connection.

10 Characteristics of Cancer Survivors

Although your doctor may not talk about it freely, spontaneous remissions do occur. In fact thousands of cases have been reported in several books such as the Spontaneous Remission Bibliography, compiled by the Institute of Noetic Sciences. Visit wwww.stayingalivecookbook.com/links.

The Centre for Integrated Healing has summarized the 10 common characteristics of those who have undergone spontaneous healing of advanced, untreatable cancer.

1. In spite of being told that their cancer is incurable they have a deep belief that their body can heal itself.

2. They take control and assume a recovery program that is unique to them. They reclaim their own responsibility rather than solely relying on experts.

3. They reconnect with spirit, awakening long hidden desires and aspirations. They reconnect with authenticity to their feelings and values and decide to live them.

4. They deepen and bring honesty to their relationships with others.

5. A complete re-assessment of their lives is undertaken. They are willing to change. This often includes diet, lifestyle, career, goals and relationships.

6. Radical changes in diet have been closely associated with spontaneous remission. These changes usually include decreasing processed, refined foods and animal fats and consuming more fruits and vegetables or becoming vegetarian.

7. They take vitamins and supplements to help support their immune system.

8. They slow down. Taking time to relax and fully enjoy the gift of life. Often prayer or meditation becomes a regular practice.

9. They become in tune with their body and "listen" for cues relating to energy, emotions and body signals that are part of daily life.

10. They rejoin with social networks and experience the joy of being of service to others. Through their own healing, they help to heal others.

Chapter Twenty One:

Common Chemicals used on produce

Common Chemicals used on produce

Organophosphate insecticides (OPs)

Methyl parathion	Apples, peaches, pears	Endocrine disrupter and neurotoxin
Methamidophos	Bell peppers, green beans, tomatoes	Endocrine disrupter and neurotoxin
Acephate	Bell peppers, green beans	Endocrine disrupter and neurotoxin
Dimethoate	Green beans, spinach	Endocrine disrupter and neurotoxin
Azinphosmethyl	Peaches, pears	Endocrine disrupter and neurotoxin
Clorpyrifos	Tomatoes	Endocrine disrupter and neurotoxin

Other Chemicals		
Oxamyl	Bell peppers	Endocrine disrupter
Dicofol	Bell peppers	Endocrine disrupter
Dieldrin	Cucumbers, winter squash	Carcinogen
Chlordane	Cucumber	Neurotoxin and suspected carcinogen
Endosulphan	Green beans	Endocrine disrupter
Iprodione	Peaches	Probable human carcinogen
Permethrin	Spinach	Possible human carcinogen
DDT	Spinach	Banned decades ago, still found as residue, can increase risk of birth defects.
Captan	Strawberries	Probable human carcinogen
Heptachlor	Winter squash	Carcinogen

Chapter Twenty Two:

Recommended Resources

Recommended Resources

All available from www.stayingalivecookbook.com/links

Centre for Integrated Healing

Suite 200, 1330 West 8th Avenue
Vancouver B.C. Canada V6H 4A6
Phone: (604) 734-7125
Fax: (604) 734-7105
Web: **www.healing.bc.ca**

TrueGreens Immune Support Formula

www.stayingalivecookbook.com/truegreens

Body Mind Spirit

All available from **www.stayingalivecookbook.com/books**

Carl Simonton

Book Titles: *Getting Well Again, Affirmations For Getting Well, The Healing Journey*

Bruce Lipton

Video Titles: *Biology of Belief*

Candice Pert

Book Titles: *Molecules of Emotion, the science behind mind-body medicine*

Institute of Noetic Sciences

Book Titles: *Spontaneous Remission Bibliography*

Health and Nutrition Books

All available from **www.stayingalivecookbook.com/books**

Physicians Committee for Responsible Medicine

Book Titles: *Healthy Eating for Life to Prevent and Treat Cancer, Eat Right Live Longer, Foods that Fight Pain*

Andrew Weil, MD

Book Titles: *8 weeks to Optimum Health, The Healthy Kitchen, Spontaneous Healing*

Alive Publishing Group

Book Titles: *Fats that Heal, Fats that Kill, Hard to Swallow - the truth about food additives, Encyclopedia of Natural Healing*

Health Quotient Questionnaire visit **www.alive.com**

Michael Murray, ND
Book Titles: *How to Prevent and Treat Cancer with Natural Medicine, Complete Book of Juicing*

Cookbooks
The Peaceful Palate, Jennifer Raymond

Moosewood Restaurant Cooks at Home, Moosewood Restaurant New Classics, Moosewood Collective and Mollie Katzen

Calciyum! R & D Bronfman

Green Door Restaurant Cookbook, Green Door Restaurant, Ottawa

The Healthy Kitchen, Andrew Weil MD, Rosie Daley

Juicing and Raw Foods Books
Complete Book of Juicing, Michael Murray ND

The Juiceman's Power of Juicing, Jay Kordich

Raw Gourmet, Nomi Shannon

Warming up to Living Foods, Elysa Markowitz

A

B

C

T

About the Author

Sally Errey, RNCP, is an acclaimed speaker on optimum health and longevity through healthy nutrition and lifestyle choices. Her 17 years of experience, combined with her love of food is reflected in her being the Nutrition Expert, Featured Chef and Food Stylist for "alive" magazine and Canada's Healthy Living Guide, as well as the Resident Nutritionist on Shaw TV's Studio 4. Sally is frequently invited to appear at Health Shows and Food Festivals.

Her company, Simple Nutrition Solutions, provides consulting services for those people seeking to manage and prevent illnesses such as diabetes, heart disease, arthritis and cancer. Currently, Sally's seminar clients include the Canadian Cancer Society, the Canadian Heart and Stroke Foundation, various corporate and Government agencies, and the University of British Columbia. Drawing on her experience of the body's immense capacity to heal, she brings vitality, a sense of adventure and humour to the field of nutrition

Sally also provides services at the Centre for Integrated Healing, a Canadian national model for providing complementary care and alternative options for those living with cancer. Her lectures, weekly cooking classes and consultations have helped to transform many people's lives.

Sally is a humorous, informative and entertaining presenter and is available to share her knowledge with your group in a seminar or cooking demonstration setting.

To contact Sally, E-mail: **happytummy@shaw.ca** or
phone (604) 734-7125 ext 234.
Visit **www.myhappytummy.com**

Consultations are available in person or by phone. Specific Nutrition protocols are available for the following:

- Weight Gain
- Detoxification and Cleansing
- Pre-surgery preparation and maximizing post surgery healing
- Increasing energy

Contact Sally today to book your appointment.

CANADIAN BOOK ORDER FORM

Please have your VISA card and mailing details ready when ordering.

Online orders:	**www.stayingalivecookbook.com**
Email orders:	**stayingalivecookbook@shaw.ca**
Fax orders:	**Toll Free 1-604-648-9436**
Postal orders:	**Belissimo Books, Box 46838, Vancouver, BC, V6J 5M4, CANADA**
Telephone orders:	**Call Toll Free 1-87-STY-ALIVE (1-877-892-5483)**

I understand that I may return any books for a full refund — for any reason, no questions asked.

Prices are in Canadian dollars and are exclusive of Government Sales Tax

Staying Alive! Cookbook for Cancer Free Living $ 29.95
Balanced Meal Wheel Kitchen Poster $ 14.95

Please send the following:

Title _____Qty ____Unit Price_____Total _____
Title _____Qty ____Unit Price_____Total _____

Sub Total _____
Add Taxes 7 % (Sub Total x 0.07)_____
Add Shipping * _____
Total Paid (CDN) _____

❏ Please send me Happy Tummy Times FREE monthly e-mail newsletter

Company Name: _____Contact Person: _____

Address 1: _____

Address 2: _____

City:_____Province:_____

Postal: _____Country: _____

Telephone: _____E-mail: _____

* Shipping: Air Mail Book rate is $5.45 each for the first TWO books and $1 for each additional book . Please phone for Surface Rates.

Payment Method: ❏ Cheque/Mail Order   ❏ Visa

Card Number _____ Exp Date ____/_____

Name on card: _____Signature _____

CALL TOLL FREE AND ORDER NOW
Toll Free 1-87-STY-ALIVE (1-877-892-5483)

US BOOK ORDER FORM

Please have your VISA card and mailing details ready when ordering.

Online orders:	**www.stayingalivecookbook.com**
Email orders:	**stayingalivecookbook@shaw.ca**
Fax orders:	**Toll Free 1-604-648-9436**
Postal orders:	**Belissimo Books, Box 46838, Vancouver, BC, V6J 5M4, CANADA**
Telephone orders:	**Call Toll Free 1-87-STY-ALIVE (1-877-892-5483)**

I understand that I may return any books for a full refund — for any reason, no questions asked.

Prices are in US dollars and are exclusive of Government Sales Tax

Staying Alive! Cookbook for Cancer Free Living	$ 21.95
Balanced Meal Wheel Kitchen Poster	$ 14.95

Please send the following:

Title _____ Qty ____ Unit Price _____ Total _____

Title _____ Qty ____ Unit Price _____ Total _____

                    Sub Total   _____
                    Add Shipping *   _____
                    Total Paid (US)   _____

❐ Please send me Happy Tummy Times FREE monthly e-mail newsletter

Company Name: _____ Contact Person: _____

Address 1: _____

Address 2: _____

City: _____ Province: _____

Postal: _____ Country: _____

Telephone: _____ E-mail: _____

* Shipping: Air Mail Book rate is $5.45 each for the first TWO books and $1 for each additional book . Please phone for Surface Rates.

Payment Method: ❐ Cheque/Mail Order   ❐ Visa

Card Number _____ Exp Date ____/_____

Name on card: _____ Signature _____

CALL TOLL FREE AND ORDER NOW
Toll Free 1-87-STY-ALIVE (1-877-892-5483)